James Hamilton, Henry Courtenay Selous

The Parable of the Prodigal Son

James Hamilton, Henry Courtenay Selous

The Parable of the Prodigal Son

ISBN/EAN: 9783744759724

Printed in Europe, USA, Canada, Australia, Japan

Cover: Foto ©ninafisch / pixelio.de

More available books at **www.hansebooks.com**

OF

THE PRODIGAL SON

WITH NOTES BY

JAMES HAMILTON, D.D., F.L.S.

AND ILLUSTRATIONS BY

HENRY COURTENAY SELOUS

LONDON

JAMES NISBET & CO. BERNERS STREET

1867

Printed by R. CLARK, *Edinburgh.*

CONTENTS.

		PAGE
THE FATHERLAND	. . .	1
LEAVING HOME .	. . . .	17
THE FAR COUNTRY	. .	33
RIOTOUS LIVING .	. . .	49
A MIGHTY FAMINE	. . . .	65
FEEDING SWINE .	. . . . .	81
A WISE RESOLUTION .	. . . .	97
A HAPPY MEETING	. . . .	113
THE BEST ROBE	.	129
THE FESTIVAL . .	. . .	145
AN ANGRY BROTHER .	. . .	161
A RIGHTEOUS FATHER	. . . . .	177
INDEX . . .	. . . . . .	193

LIST OF ILLUSTRATIONS.

DESIGNED BY HENRY COURTENAY SELOUS.

ENGRAVED BY G. PEARSON.

———◆◆◆——

A certain man had two sons . . . . *To face page* 3

The younger of them said to his father, Father, give me the portion of goods that falleth to me 19

The younger son gathered all together, and took his journey into a far country 35

The younger son . . . . took his journey into a far country, and there wasted his substance with riotous living 51

He went and joined himself to a citizen of that country ; and he sent him into his fields to feed swine 67

He would fain have filled his belly with the husks that the swine did eat . 83

When he was yet a great way off, his father saw him . . . 99

His father ran, and fell on his neck, and kissed him . . . 115

Bring forth the best robe and put it on him ; and put a ring on his hand, and shoes on his feet 131

For this my son was dead, and is alive again ; he was lost, and is found.   And they began to be merry 147

Thy brother is come ; and thy father hath killed the fatted calf, because he hath received him safe and sound . . . 163

He was angry, and would not go in : therefore came his father out, and entreated him 179

THE FATHERLAND.

B

"A certain man had two sons."—LUKE xv. 2.

A CERTAIN MAN HAD TWO SONS.

THE FATHERLAND.

OUR cords are clumsy. Strand by strand, and rope by rope, we twist our cables; yet we dare not lengthen them too far, for fear their own weight break them, and in the strain of the tempest the strongest fly asunder like flax in flame. God spins his cords so fine that, except in diffracted light, you cannot see them; but these cords of His are seldom broken. You befriend a youth or relieve a stranger, and you think no more about it; till on a distant day, perhaps in a foreign land, in some hour of need, help is raised up, and in your deliverer you recognise the object of your former bounty. And just as in such an instance, held by a mystic clue, the little seed which you cast on the waters comes back into your bosom a loaf of bread; so the old saying also holds true, and "curses come home to roost." A crime is committed, and all trace is obliterated, every token buried; but now that the head which holds the fatal secret is laid on a dying pillow, the leash is pulled, and dark and croaking descends the bird of evil omen, or with fiery eye and crimson beak the vulture of despair, and with fear of coming judgment scares the guilty conscience.

Of all God's cords the finest, and perhaps the strongest, is the cord of love. Quitting his native chimney, among the canals and grassy fields of Holland, the stork pursues the retiring summer, and soon overtakes it in Nubia or Morocco. There, quite unconscious of the fetter beneath his wing, he revels on the snakes of Taurus or the frogs of Nile : till at last, on a brilliant May morning, there is a sharp tug, and then a long steady pull, and high overhead float the broad pinions, and presently in the streets of Haarlem the boys look up, and shout their welcome, as, with eager haste and noisy outcry, an old acquaintance drops down upon the gable, and, drawn back to the old anchorage by a hawser of a thousand miles, the feathery sails are once more furled. Like instinct over a generation's interval brings back the exile to his Highland glen. It matters not that in the soft Bermudas life is luxury ; it is of no avail that in this Canadian clearing a rosy household has sprung up and in proud affection clings around him ; towards the haunts of his childhood there is a strange deep-hidden yearning, which often sends absent looks towards northern stars, and ends at last in the actual pilgrimage. And although by the time of his return he finds that no money can buy back the ancestral abode ; although, as he crosses the familiar hill and opens the sunny strath, strange solitude meets him ; although when he comes up, the hamlet is roofless and silent, and the bonny beild, the nest of his boyhood, a ruin ; although behind the cold hearth rank nettles wave, and from the cairn covering the spot where in the mornings of another world he waked up so cosily, young weasels peep forth ; although the plane is cut down, or the bourtree, under whose sabbatic shadow his father used at eventide to meditate ; although where the vision dissolves a pang must remain, there is no need that he should go back, bleak and embittered, as to a disenchanted world. This glut of reality was wanted to quench a long fever : but even here, if his own heart is true, he will find that God's cord is not broken. Cottages dissolve and family circles scatter, but piety and love cannot perish. The cord is not broken ; it is only the mooring-post which a friendly hand has moved farther inland, and fixed sure and stedfast within the veil ; and as the strain which used to pull along the level is now drawing upward, the home which memory used to picture in the Highlands, faith learns to seek in Heaven.

We too were once at home. As even pagan Cleanthes and Aratus sang—

" We too are God's offspring."*

The race opened its existence under the eye of God, made after his image ; and whether he exercised his

---

* The well-known expression quoted and endorsed by St. Paul in his address to the Athenians, Acts xvii. 28, 29. Like Paul, Aratus, who flourished about 270 B.C., was a native of Cilicia. His poem, the *Phænomena*, opens with an acknowledgment of Zeus, and our dependence upon him, and derivation from him :

Πάντη δὲ Διὸς κεχρήμεθα πάντες·
Τοῦ γὰρ καὶ γένος ἐσμέν.

gentle dominion, or was occupied among the trees of the garden, or walked with his heavenly Father, listening to His voice in the cool of the day, nothing could be nobler or more blessed than that imperial infancy. Nor have we quite forgotten it. Betwixt what the Book has told us, and what is recalled by a dim mysterious memory, we feel that times are changed with us. We once were better off. A love smiled over us, a glory shone around us, which never meets us now; and many of our dearest words—Love, Joy, Innocence—seem to be so much a reminiscence of a far-off, long-faded time, that we may be excused for standing still and asking in bewilderment—

> " Have we been all at fault ?   Are we the sons
> Of pilgrim sires who left their lovelier land ?
> And do we call inhospitable climes
> By names they brought from home ?"*

The true home of humanity is God,—God trusted, communed with, beloved, obeyed; and

> " Not in entire forgetfulness,
> And not in utter nakedness,"

do we come " from God, who is our home," but "trailing clouds of glory with us."† Alloyed and interrupted by much that is base and wicked, there are in human nature still touches of tenderness, gleams of good feeling, noble impulses, momentary visitations of a natural piety,

---

* *Balder*, p. 181.

† Wordsworth's " Intimations of Immortality."

brought away from that better time and its blest abode, and which may be regarded as electric thrills along the line which connects with its Creator a fallen but redeemed humanity : as so many gentle checks of that golden chain which will one day bring back God's banished, and see the world "all righteous."

Far from home, humanity is still in the hand of God. Not only is it subject to His righteous and irresistible sovereignty, but it has a place in his deep and desirous compassion.   And for every one of us it is a solemn and affecting thought, that before he can be finally and for ever lost, he must "break the band and cast away the cord" by which forgiving mercy would draw him to itself. We know that it too often happens. Too often do we see men turn the back to God and not the face ; and the last glance we get of them they are still departing. Still averse from God, and still departing, the cord of love and life's brittle thread snap together ; and passing the bourne beyond which is " outer darkness," there is nothing which we are allowed to hope for them in that world where no gospel follows and no Holy Spirit strives. But, on the other hand, where there is any relenting towards the Ever-blessed, what can be more encouraging than the assurance that in the case of our fallen family, much as sin abounds, grace much more abounds ? and that, notwithstanding all we have done to forfeit the filial position, there is on God's side so much of fatherly affection as not only to desire our return, but to devise methods unprecedented and costly for bringing us back ?

The head of the great household is God, and the earthly home He has constituted so as to be an image of his own paternity. That home is founded in love, and in administering it love is called forth every day,—often a pitying, forbearing, forgiving love,—a love sometimes severe and frowning, often self-denying, it may chance self-sacrificing. As the world now is—a ruin, with a remedial scheme in the midst of it—that home is the nearest image of the church, and should be the most efficient fellow-worker with it. " In the family the first man himself would receive lessons on self-government such as even the garden of Eden did not supply, and perpetual occasion for its exercise. In what a variety of ways would he learn to repeat to his children the substance of the divine prohibition to himself—' Thou shalt not eat of it.' How soon would he who had had paradise for a home discover that if he would convert home into a paradise he must guard his offspring at this point, subordinating their lower propensities to their superior powers."* If presided over by those who themselves fear God—and otherwise no house is a home—there will be something sacred in its atmosphere, and alike enforced by affection and authority the lessons of heavenly wisdom will sink deep ; and with a sufficient probation superadded to a careful protection, it is to be

* Harris's *Patriarchy*, p. 113.

hoped that, before transplantation into the world's rough weather, good dispositions may have been so far confirmed as only to strengthen by further trial.

We must not be too confident. It would be rash to say that where the home is right the inmates never can go wrong. There was once a great heart-break in heaven : angels grieved, for so many of their brethren had gone away to return no more. Since then, another great prodigal has left the Father's house—for of all prodigals our race is the greatest. And when the Great Father has himself had to mourn over wayward runaway children, let us fence our habitations as we please, it would be too much to hope that evil shall never enter, or that headstrong folly shall never gather all together and go away.

Still, the promise to believers includes their children, and the instances are anomalous and few where a hopeful outset ends in a worthless old age. In seeking for your offspring the kingdom of heaven and the righteousness thereof, you who are parents may confidently claim the sympathy of the Father of spirits, and the succour of that great Teacher who has all hearts in his hand, and turns them as the rivers of water are turned. And the records of religious biography nearly all confirm the promise. The favoured Samuel is the son of the praying Hannah. The young evangelist is the child of the believing Eunice, and Eunice, again, is the daughter of the like-minded Lois. The God of Abraham, Isaac, and

Jacob is the God of Joseph also. The first martyr in
the days of the bloody Mary was John Rogers. He is
still represented by honourable and Christian descend-
ants in this country; and in the United States, where his
children's children have reached the eleventh generation,
it has been remarked that few families contain so many
pious members, and singularly enough, with one inter-
mission, the eldest son has always been a minister.
Having frequently heard the remark that the sons of
ministers and deacons turn out badly, the secretary of
the Massachusetts Sabbath School Society instituted an
inquiry in a district where he could insure correct returns.
It contained 268 families of the class in question, and in
these there were 1290 young persons above fifteen years
of age. Out of these 1290 young people 884 were hope-
fully pious, and the great majority (794) were united to
the church of Christ. Amongst these households there
were 56 highly-favoured families, with an aggregate
grown-up membership of 249 individuals, where all were
hopefully pious. On the other hand, out of the 1290
only 17 had become dissipated, and most of these had
broken down whilst away from home.*

In order to make your home the preparation for
heaven, the first thing is to strengthen that cord of love
by which you ought to hold your child, even as our
heavenly Father holds his children. That love is yours
already—an upleaping, uplooking affection, if you do not

* Barnes on Isaiah lix. 21.

destroy its tenderness by perpetual rebuffs, if you do not forfeit reverence by being yourself unworthy of it. " Ye fathers, provoke not your children to wrath;" be not always scolding, reproving, punishing; "but bring them up in the nurture and admonition of the Lord." Take advantage of their affection for yourself, and use it as the appointed medium for drawing them into the love of God. When the soft iron is in the electric circuit it grows magnetic, and not only clings itself, but keeps lesser and kindred masses clinging : so when the soul is in the right relation to the living God, it acquires a strong induction—a mighty power of attracting others in the same direction. If your conduct is consistent—if your life goes by God's rules—power from on high will attend the occasional word or the special effort. Long lectures and formal advices are of small avail ; but should there occur some solemnising season—a time of deepened spiritual earnestness—a time when your own soul is melted by the love of Christ—a time when your boy him-self is brought to unwonted tenderness, by sickness or sorrow, or a departure from home ;—if at such a season you should speak to him fully, affectionately, seriously, like the last charge of David to Solomon, like Israel's farewell to his sons, a peculiar power and pathos will attend the words, and will secure the preservation of a father's legacy.

Meanwhile, the precept is plain, the duty clear. Train up the child in the way he should go. If he is not

to go in the way of low pastime and coarse indulgence,
point him to higher joys ; open to him the well-spring of
knowledge ; try to ascertain and develope a turn for
some ennobling pursuit, or create a taste for the treasures
bequeathed by genius. If he is not to go in the way of
sinners—if you would preserve him from the temptations
of idleness and the vacuity of an aimless existence—
train him up in some craft or calling ; let him go forth
into society fit to do, and to do well, some portion or other
of that work of which the world has need, and which
makes so sweet the bread and so pleasant the rest of the
labourer. If he is not to go in the way that leadeth to
destruction, make it plain that you would rather see him
good than great ; and, yourself in the fear of God all
the day, train him up in the way of simplicity and godly
sincerity. Train him up in frugal tastes and self-deny-
ing habits—if possible with a Roman hardihood of
frame, and as much as may be with a Spartan disdain of
luxury. Train him up in energy and self-reliance, grap-
pling with difficulties, and learning independence by
doing things for himself. Train him up in manly frank-
ness, that with open face he may meet each friendly
overture,—in modesty withal, lest a precocious arrogance
repel the wise, lest his own mental growth be stunted by
a supercilious priggishness. Train him up in the way
of universal good-will and general helpfulness, so that
wherever there is a burden to be borne he may lend a
hand ; so that wherever there is a friendly service to be

done he may have an errand ; so that gratitude, affection, and the blessing of them that were ready to perish, may surround his goings, and then embalm his memory.

After all, however, there is another influence which goes farther in creating the home. It is mother-love which endears the fatherland, and it is to the cradle that the fairy-line is fastened which even in the far country holds so mysteriously the heart of the wanderer.

When Napoleon, with his army of invasion, lay at Boulogne, an English sailor who had been captured tried to escape in a little raft or skiff which he had patched together with bits of wood and the bark of trees. Hearing of his attempt, the First Consul ordered him to be brought into his presence, and asked if he really meant to cross the Channel in such a crazy contrivance. "Yes, and if you will let me, I am still willing to try." "You must have a sweetheart whom you are so anxious to revisit." "No," said the young man, "I only wish to see my mother, who is old and infirm." "And you shall see her," was the reply, "and take to her this money from me ; for she must be a good mother who has such an affectionate son." And orders were given to send the sailor with a flag of truce on board the first British cruiser which came near enough.*

Napoleon was always eager to declare his own obligations to his high-spirited and courageous mother, the

---

* The story is told by Alison (*French Revolution*, ch. lxxxi.), who quotes Las Casas. It has been turned into verse by T. Campbell.

beautiful Letizia Ramolini ; but the difficulty would be to
find any man of mark who has not made the same avowal.*
Of a few biographical works lying near at this moment,
five out of six begin to the same tenor. Take an in-
stance or two. The first is Kirby, long the patriarch of
English entomology. " To his mother, and to her alone,
he did not hesitate to affirm that he was indebted for his
taste for natural history." While still a little child she
gave him, as his most precious playthings, shells from an
old family cabinet. He was exceedingly attracted by
their different shapes and colours, and soon learned to
know them every one, and ask for them by their right
names ; and when a veteran of eighty-four he still showed
his friends a little herbarium which with the help of his
dear mother he had compiled at nine years of age.† Next
comes Goethe. His mother " is one of the pleasantest
figures in German literature. Her simple, hearty, joy-
ous, and affectionate nature endeared her to all. . . She
had read most of the best German and Italian authors, had
picked up considerable desultory information, and had
that ' mother-wit' which so often in women and poets
seems to render culture superfluous. . . To Wolfgang she
transmitted her love of story-telling, her animal spirits,
her love of everything which bore the stamp of distinctive
individuality, and her love of seeing happy faces round

---

* Perhaps we should except Napoleon's great rival ; see the article on
Wellington in the *Quarterly Review* for July 1866.
† Freeman's *Life of the Rev. W. Kirby*, pp. 17, 18.

her." * The last is the great critic and grammarian, Thiersch. His mother did not teach him Greek, but out of her Lutheran hymn-book she taught him songs about the Saviour and His dying love. She also taught him kindness to the poor,—a lesson which all through life he practised liberally. On one occasion, whilst a small boy, his mother left him at home with the door locked and the window open. A beggar woman came. There was a French crown on the table, which little Fritz at once handed out to her, bidding her tenderly " Come soon back again." She was so honest as not to go away till the lady returned, and for restoring the crown was rewarded with cakes and eight good groschen.†

Yes, if you choose, let the foundation be granite, let heart of oak be the roof-tree. Let masculine energy, stern rectitude, unflinching endurance build up the paternal abode ; and assign to the head of the house such intelligence, elevation, dignity, as beseem " the father and the priest." But for the cheerful plenishing, for that warm inner atmosphere in which childhood nestles, and in which good feelings are fostered into life, for those first and most influential lessons which precede all teachers and tutors, you must look to a kindlier and more pervasive presence ; you must think of one who is more than either housewife or learned lady. With calm, clear eyes, deep insight, ready sympathy ; active, without bustle ;

* G. H. Lewes's *Life of Goethe*, pp. 7, 8.
† Fr. Thiersch's *Leben* (1866), vol. i. p. 3.

alert, without over-anxious vigilance ; ignorant perchance
of æsthetic rules, yet with subtile touches transforming
into a fine picture the home-spun canvas, and with a soft
fairy music blending into harmony the noises of the
day; apathetic about stocks and shares and far-off
millions, but with a keen appreciation of new sovereigns
and no disdain for sixpences ; a mere formalist, if pro-
fessing interest in city improvements or parochial reforms,
but as touching torn curtains and threadbare carpets much
exercised in spirit ; sure that the commotions of Europe
will all come right, but shedding bitter tears at any out-
break of juvenile waywardness, and praying earnestly,
"Oh, that Ishmael may live before thee !" with small belief
in the transcendental philosophy, and allowing that much
may be said on both sides, but in the interpretation of the
Ten Commandments positive, unreasoning, absolute ; in
theology hopelessly confounding the distinctions of the
schools, and in an innocent way adopting half the heresies,
but drinking direct from the fountain that living water
which others prefer chalybeate through the iron pipe or
aerated from the filtering-pond, and in a style which
Calvin and Grotius might equally envy teaching the little
ones the love of the Saviour ;—the angel in the house
moulds a family for heaven, and by dint of holy example
and gentle control her early and most efficacious ministry
goes farther than any other to lay the foundations of
future excellence, and train up sons and daughters for the
Lord Almighty.

LEAVING HOME.

C

" The younger son gathered all together, and took his journey."—LUKE xv. 13.

THE YOUNGER OF THEM SAID TO HIS FATHER, "FATHER, GIVE ME THE
PORTION OF GOODS THAT FALLETH TO ME."

LEAVING HOME.

SELDOM, it may be hoped, does a youth leave home simply because he has tired of it; still more rarely, we trust, because he wishes to lead a life of mere self-indulgence. One instance, however, of this kind we do remember, with its unlooked-for ending. In the town of Huntly there was living, a hundred years ago, a lad lately returned from college, whose only quarrel with a rough and regardless neighbourhood was the insufficient scope it gave to his love of fun and frolic. Having heard a great deal about London, and believing that it was the place where every man might do that which is good in his own eyes, he gathered all together, and took his journey towards the southern capital. On the road, however, he turned aside to visit a kinsman who had himself led a life of notorious wickedness, but whose friendship he wished to retain. This relative he found on a bed of sickness; but although his bodily sufferings were great, they were almost swallowed up in the anguish of his spirit. In a fearful tide of remorse, his sinful life came surging back upon his memory, and as God's waves and billows went over him loud were the

cries for mercy and vehement the promises of amend-
ment, which he offered in every gasping interval. God
spared him. Eventually he recovered; and recovering,
he returned to the old excess of riot. But though he
forgot his own vows and prayers, his visitor could not
forget them—the outcries of a guilty conscience shaken
over the mouth of hell. Not only did they drive all
thoughts of folly from his mind, but they sent him back
to his own abode a crushed and frightened penitent.
At last, having obtained mercy, he startled his fellow-
townsmen by standing up in the market-place and
urging them to flee from the wrath to come; and
although at first scoffs and derision—yes, and angry
missiles—were his recompense, through a long life he
persisted snatching brands from the burning, and giving
numbers in Banff and Moray reason to bless his solemn
and rousing ministrations.*

More frequently it is on an honourable errand that
the youthful pilgrim sets forth. A subsistence must be

---

* The above particulars were related to us in 1840 by an "old
disciple" in Huntly, James Maitland, who well remembered George
Cowie, and who, we believe, was one of the fruits of his ministry.
Describing the rough treatment given to the young evangelist, our
informant said—"They flung *custocks* at him;" and many of our
readers will remember the old song which associates "custocks"
(cabbage-stems) with Strathbogie. In a brief memoir it is mentioned
that Mr. Cowie's "first alarm about his soul was occasioned by
witnessing the death of an uncle in the year 1765" (Kinniburgh's
Fathers of Independency in Scotland, p. 13). Our impression is, that
the uncle temporarily recovered.

earned, an education must be obtained, a profession has
been chosen, a divine call is obeyed; and so the student
goes to college, the recruit seeks his regiment, the sailor
joins his ship, the aspirant after an honourable independ-
ence starts for the city or the distant colony; and there
is on both sides true tenderness—on the one side the
best intention, on the other many an earnest prayer.
" Happy, thrice happy, as an after-remembrance, be the
final parting between hopeful son and fearful parent, at
the foot of that mystic bridge which starts from the
threshold of home—lost in the dimness of the far-
opposing shore—bridge over which goes the boy who
shall never return but as the man."*

Blessed be God, the tearful hopes of that anxious
moment are often fulfilled; and happy are the parents
who, in the frank and affectionate communications of
their absent child, see plainly that the heart is still at
home; and still happier they who, after whatsoever
interval, receive him back with new excellence developed
or with character confirmed. To John Angell James's
mother it was a delightful discovery when the careless
apprentice returned to Blandford and she found a Bible
in his great-coat pocket. A bundle of bank-notes would
not have made her near so happy. How the eyes of
Henry Kirke White's mother must have filled over
these lines from her gifted son near the close of his
Cambridge career:—" Never do I lay myself on my bed

* Lord Lytton's *What will he do with it?* vol. ii. p. 84.

before you have all passed before me in my prayers;
and one of my first earthly wishes is to make you com-
fortable, and provide that rest and quiet for your mind
which you so much need. I shall have some quiet
parsonage, where you may come and spend the summer
months. Maria and Kate will then be older, and you
will be less missed." And when the bitterness of death
was over—for even though a sword should pierce through
the soul, blessed among women is the martyr's mother*—
still more blessed may we deem in after-years that devout
lady in Manchester, who, in the June of 1555, received this
letter from her son in London, looking forward to his fiery
chariot at Smithfield :—" I die as a witness of Christ, his
gospel and truth, which hitherto I have confessed as well
by preaching as by imprisonment; and now, even pre-
sently, I shall confirm the same by fire. I send all my
writings to you by my brother Roger : do with them as
you will, because I cannot as I would. I pray God to
bless you and keep you from evil. May He give you
patience, may He make you thankful for me and for
yourself, that He will take your child to witness His
verity. . . . Thus, my dear mother, I take my last
farewell of you in this life; beseeching the almighty and
eternal Father, by Christ, to grant us to meet in the life
to come, where we shall give Him continual thanks and
praise Him for ever and ever. Out of prison, your son
in the Lord, JOHN BRADFORD."

* Luke ii. 35 ; i. 28, 42.

For character there is a twofold security—the first commandment and the fifth—love to God and hallowed domestic affections: nor is that character likely to drift where both anchors are out, and where the heart is well moored both to the home on earth and the home on high. Reader, have you both? Young men, scattered about in little companies or dwelling alone in your solitary lodging, have you both? Like a good ship off a dangerous coast, are you keeping your heart with all diligence, and are both bower and sheet anchor out? the bower of memory binding you to the fireside far away where loved ones linger? the sheet-anchor of hope entering within the veil, and attaching to the Father's house and the goodly fellowship assembled there? Inasmuch as both homes are lost to sight, they are in your case things of faith; but in the storm of temptation, when the importunities of sense and the enticements of Satan are equally vehement, the only preservative from shipwreck is faith in the unseen— faithful memory or faithful hope; and when the poor little kedge of carnal policy comes home—when like a leaden fluke good humour bends, like a rotten cable worldly wisdom snaps in sunder—they are only God's anchors which continue sure and steadfast.

To those who are still in the outset of their active life we offer a few further hints. They will be received in good part, for they are given by one who still remembers some of his own youthful feelings, and who has often had reason to rejoice in the good and gallant fight of young men who were "strong and overcame the wicked one."

If you wish to have a happy and honourable career, you must choose the best companions. Your fellow-clerks, your neighbours in the shop or factory, you cannot choose : they are chosen for you : but it is left in your own option to select your friends ; and you may find it a great difficulty. If you were a dry, disagreeable fellow, people would let you alone ; but if you are worth cultivating ; if instead of being a proser or a pedant, you have pleasant dispositions and a frank, popular way ; instead of being a silent solemn automaton, or the next thing to it, a man of one idea—a wooden centaur who has grown into the same substance with his hobby ; if you have a rich and varied nature ; if you have humour ; if you are musical ; if you are fond of athletic sports ; if you read ; if you row ;—every separate liking is just a several hook, a distinct affinity to which a kindred spirit will be apt to attach itself, and ere ever you are aware you may find yourself complicated with an acquaintanceship which, although at some point or other agreeable, is on the whole cumbrous or uncongenial. It is pleasant to feel that you are liked, and it is painful to keep at arm's length those who take to you and would evidently value your society. Nor would it be fair to call them by hard names. They are not seducers or systematic assassins, lying in wait for the precious soul ; and the harm they do is not so much from having any evil purpose as from their having no right

principle. Nevertheless, if a man carrying contagion pro-
poses a visit or offers you his arm, although he intends
no injury, you stand aloof, and you are not to be de-
nounced as a churl for declining a danger which he does
not realise. And in the philharmonic class or in the rifle
corps, you are alongside of a splendid shot or an excellent
singer, and you are not a little drawn to one another; but
if on nearer intercourse it turns out that he drinks too
freely, or keeps no Sabbath, or has loose notions on
morality—"can a man take coals into his bosom and not
be burned?" "the companion of fools shall be destroyed"
—it would not be complaisance but cowardice—it would
be a sinful softness, which allowed affinity in taste to
imperil your faith or your virtue. It would be the same
sort of courtesy which in the equatorial forest, for the
sake of its beautiful leaf, lets the liana with its strangling
arms run up the plantain or orange, and pays the forfeit
in blasted boughs and total ruin. It would be the same
sort of courtesy which, for fear of appearing rude or in-
hospitable, took into dock the infected vessel, or welcomed,
not as a patient but a guest, the plague-stricken stranger.

A great help is a good companion. Robert Story
and Thomas Pringle were lads of seventeen who from
the same pleasant Roxburghshire went up to Edinburgh
College sixty years ago. They "lodged in the same
rooms, where amidst the novelties of the capital they con-
tinued to 'remember their Creator in the days of their
youth.' They performed religious service regularly, as

they had been accustomed to see it done at home, taking
the duty alternately. The Sabbath they kept holy, as
they had been taught to do ; avoiding so much as open-
ing a book on that day which was not of a directly re-
ligious character."* To the nobler attributes nothing is
so fatal as fast living, and with the pure innocent lives
which these young friends led it was wonderful how rich
in romance was the rest of existence, how rich withal in
religious feeling. That fine idealism which, added to
faith, gives the soul two pinions and makes the sublimest
spirits, was never broken in the case of either, and they
could not only soar at will, but—as long as you continue
a little child you keep the sceptre, you retain the kingdom
of heaven—in virtue of their very unworldliness, they had
strange ascendency over men. The one, a cripple and a
man of letters, inspired his own family with enthusiasm
such as clansmen used to feel for stalwart chieftain, and
in the make-believe of his genius the South-African glen
to which he carried them off wanted no Tweed in order to
resemble the Border, whilst from his gentle goodness
there fell on Bushman and Caffre a reverence and a re-
spect for his little settlement not to be gained by the
musket and cannon. The other we still remember with
lustrous eyes wide open to the beauties of the landscape,
but in his inner daily walk expatiating through scenes far
fairer : weak in that logic in which Scotchmen are strong,
but strong in that love and devotion without which school

Leitch Ritchie's *Memoirs of T. Pringle*, p. xvii.

logic is weak : the pastor of Roseneath, a brightly-cloudy
pillar, transcendental and indefinite, but irradiated at
top by a sun which to his spirit all these forty years had
never set : with a creed not the clearest, but with a
Christ-loving heart, moving on before his people in a
way which made them feel that if they could only follow
the same shining track, they too would reach the better
land.*

Two are better than one, and you will find it both pro-
tection and incentive if you can secure a faithful friend ;
and in some respects better than two are the many :
therefore you cannot do more wisely than seek out in the
Young Men's Society a wider companionship; and whilst
instructed by the information of some, and strengthened
by the firmer faith or larger experience of others, there
are important themes on which you will learn to think
with precision, and in the exercise of public speaking you
will either acquire a useful talent or will turn it to good
account.

You are a young man away from home. We have
said, Choose good companions ; we must add, Beware of
bad habits.

---

* Some one called Pringle "a Scot without guile." See Beattie's
Life of Thomas Campbell, vol. ii. p. 56. His effort to secure " homes
abroad" for his kinsfolk by carrying them out to South Africa is an in-
teresting chapter in the history of emigration, and from his venerable
widow, long an attached member of Regent Square congregation, the
author has heard many anecdotes of lion-hunts and other incidents of
life at Glen Lynden.

It was the third hour of the day, and Abdallah still lingered over the morning repast, when there came a little fly and alighted on the rim of his goblet. It sipped a particle of syrup and was gone. It came next morning, and the next, and the next again, till it caught the eye of the scholar. As he considered it, and as it gave forth its many colours and moved itself aright, it seemed beautiful exceedingly, and in his heart he could not find to drive it away. Wherefore it came day by day continually, and waxing bolder and bolder it withal became greater and greater, till in the size as of a locust could be perceived as the likeness of a man; and the greater that it grew the more winning were its ways, frisking like a sunbeam, singing like a peri, so that the eyes of the simple one were blinded, and in all this he did not perceive the subtlety of an evil jinn. Wherefore, waxing bolder and yet bolder, whatsoever of dainty meats its soul desired the lying spirit freely took, and when, waxing wroth, the son of the prophet said, " This is my daily portion from the table of the mufti ; there is not enough for thee and me ;" playing one of its pleasant tricks, the brazen-faced deceiver caused the simple one to smile ; until in process of time the scholar perceived that as his guest waxed stronger and stronger, he himself waxed weaker and weaker.

Now also there arose frequent contention between the demon and his dupe, and the youth smote the demon so sore that it departed for a season. Thereupon Abdallah rejoiced exceedingly, and said, "I have triumphed over mine enemy, and when it seemeth good in my sight I shall smite him that he die." But after not many days, lo and behold! the jinn came again, arrayed in goodly garments, and bringing a present in its hand, and with its fair speech, saying, "Is it not a little one?" it enticed this silly dove so that he again received it into his chamber.

On the morrow, when Abdallah came not into the assembly of studious youth, the mufti said, "Wherefore tarrieth the son of the faithful? perchance he sleepeth." Therefore they resorted even to his chamber, and knocked, and lifted up their voice; but as he made no answer the mufti opened the door, and behold! on the divan lay the dead body of his disciple. His visage was black and swollen, and on his throat was the pressure of a finger broader than the palm of a mighty man. All the stuff belonging to the hapless one was gone, the gold and the jewels, and the parchment-rolls, and the changes of raiment; and in the soft earth of the garden were discerned the footsteps of a giant. The mufti measured one of the prints, and lo! it was six cubits long.

What means the apologue? who can expound the riddle? Is it the bottle or the betting-book? is it the billiard-table? is it the theatre, or the tea-garden, or the music-saloon? is it laziness? is it debt? is it the wasted Sunday? But know that an evil habit is an elf constantly expanding. It may come in at the key-hole, but it will soon grow too big for the house. At first it

may seem too trivial for serious attack, but it will pre-
sently prove the death of the owner. We know not that
we can give a better commentary than the experience of
a citizen of Boston, whose kindly memory is still hon-
oured in New England. Writing to a young friend,
says Amos Lawrence: "At the commencement of your
journey take this for your motto, that the difference of
going *just right* or *a little wrong* will be the difference
of finding yourself in good quarters or in a miserable
bog or slough at the end of it. Of the whole number
educated in the Groton stores for some years before and
after myself, no one else, to my knowledge, escaped the
bog or slough; and my escape I trace to the simple fact of
my having put a restraint upon my appetite. We five boys
were in the habit, every forenoon, of making a drink
compounded of rum, raisins, etc., with biscuit—all palat-
able to eat and drink. After being in the store four
weeks I found myself admonished by my appetite of the
approach of the hour for indulgence. Thinking the
habit might make trouble if allowed to grow stronger,
without further apology to my seniors I declined partak-
ing with them. My first resolution was to abstain for a
week, and, when the week was out, for a month, and
then for a year. Finally, I resolved to abstain for the
rest of my apprenticeship, which was for five years
longer. During that whole period I never drank a
spoonful, though I mixed gallons daily for my old master
and his customers. I decided not to be a slave to to-

bacco in any form, though I loved the odour of it then, and even now have in my drawer a superior Havannah cigar, given me not long since by a friend, but only to smell at. I have never in my life smoked a cigar; never chewed but one quid, and that was before I was fifteen; and never took an ounce of snuff, though the scented rappee of forty years ago had great charms for me. Now, I say to this simple fact of starting *just right*, am I indebted, with God's blessing on my labours, for my present position, as well as that of the numerous connections sprung up around me."*

It is of vast moment to be "just right" when starting. At Preston, at Malines, at many such places, the lines go gently asunder; so fine is the angle that at first the paths are almost parallel, and it seems of small moment which you select. But a little farther on one of them turns a corner or dives into a tunnel, and now that the speed is full the angle opens up, and at the rate of a mile a minute the divided convoy flies asunder: one passenger is on the way to Italy, another to the swamps of Holland; one will step out in London, the other in the Irish Channel. It is not enough that you book for the better country: you must keep the way, and a small deviation may send you entirely wrong. A slight deflection from honesty, a slight divergence from perfect truthfulness, from perfect sobriety, may throw you on a wrong track altogether, and make a failure of that life

* *Diary and Correspondence of Amos Lawrence,* Boston, p. 10.

which should have proved a comfort to your family, a
credit to your country, a blessing to mankind.

Beware of the bad habit. It makes its first appear-
ance as a tiny fay, and is so innocent, so playful, so
minute, that none save a precisian would denounce it, and
it seems hardly worth while to whisk it away. The trick
is a good joke, the lie is white, the glass is harmless, the
theft is only a few apples from a farmer's orchard, the
bet is only sixpence, the debt is only half-a-crown. But
the tiny fay is capable of becoming a tremendous giant;
and if you connive and harbour him, he will nourish him-
self at your expense, and then, springing on you as an
armed man, will drag you down to destruction.

THE FAR COUNTRY.

D

" A certain man had two sons : and the younger of them said to his father, Father, give me the portion of goods that falleth to me. And he divided unto them his living. And not many days after, the younger son gathered all together, and took his journey into a far country, and there wasted his substance with riotous living."
—LUKE xv. 11-13.

THE YOUNGER SON GATHERED ALL TOGETHER, AND TOOK HIS JOURNEY
INTO A FAR COUNTRY.

THE FAR COUNTRY.

As it rises up to our imagination, there was once a pleasant home presided over by a kind and wealthy householder. Two sons grew up in it. The oldest was sedate and prudent; so correct and proper that he seldom got into any trouble, and was always well pleased with himself. But we should not wonder though the younger was more popular. Not near so diligent, he had a fine flow of spirit, and with his sallies of fancy and his frank hearty ways, we can believe that he was his mother's favourite, and that when he turned up among the labourers in the harvest-field, his coming would be the signal for shouts and merriment.

Fancy is a famous inmate, but singing out of doors she becomes a dangerous decoy. Precious beyond rubies is the idealism which can invest with celestial dignity the earthly avocation, and which, even when the hands are engaged in downright drudgery, can fill the mind with noble thoughts, and carry you through the daily task as a son or daughter of the king; but very perilous is this same power when, instead of dignifying duty and bringing heaven into the home, she becomes the syren, and, flying out at the window, sings on the distant hill or far off at sea, luring you away from the solid land or the sober threshold.

So was it with the younger son. The father's house grew tame. To be doing the same things over and over again, day after day, was very tiresome. He would like more liberty; he would like to see the world. Tush! why talk of danger? That is the way old people always do; but he is out of leading-strings. He is no longer a baby. He is come of age, and can take care of himself : and what is more, he is his own master, and entitled to do as he pleases. And so, with the song of the charmer hardening his heart against every delicate or duteous consideration, practically avowing that home has lost its attractions, and that he does not mean to waste any more years " serving his father," he goes up and demands his inheritance. " Father, give me the portion of goods that falleth to me." Nor does it appear that the father refused. Man is a free agent. If Gabriel will not continue in heaven as a son, he shall not be detained as a slave; and when Gabriel's younger brother, Adam, wearied of obedience, wished to set up for himself, " the portion of goods which fell to him" he was allowed to take with him---those bodily organs, those senses, those intellectual and moral endowments, which in Eden were an inexhaustible fortune, but which in the " far country" go but a little way.

A few days intervened. For converting into gold and gems his goods and chattels, so as to make them portable, some little delay was needful; nor does the bird always take wing the instant the cage is opened. As he was getting his own way, he would take his own time; and as he was free to set off when he pleased, he did not need to be anxious or hurried.

At last it arrived, the much-wished-for morning. No mention is made of any tender leave-taking; for when a man becomes a lover of pleasure his affections get utterly blunted. The tears of a mother are troublesome. He would rather that people would not make so much ado, but show a little more sense. And so, without a word of thanks to his father, without any keepsake to his old companions, he hied away on the eventful journey.

Do you not see him? Healthy and handsome, and flushed with hope, he trips along gaily. With pearls and rubies in his purse, and such a load of coin in his girdle, who could be richer? And as up its south-eastern portal he presses into the sunland, life swims before him a vision of glory, a romance of ever-varying ecstasy. Tasks are over; care is left behind; the swallow in its lofty sweep is not more free; the butterfly, tipsy with nectar and dozing on the acacia blooms, is not more happy. O life, life! What a sensation is the fresh feel of existence! It is dull work to walk. He must jump for joy. He must run up the steep places. He must shout to the jerboas and the conies, and send them

helter-skelter to their holes.   In merry mischief he must
chase the wild hog and her squealing litter till they
reach their refuge in the reeds or the jungle ; and in
mad freaks and frolicsome escapades he flings away

> " The prodigal excess
> Of too familiar happiness."

Till now, he is in a new land.   It seems all garden.
Palms are plentiful, and orange-trees, with rich exotic
scent and golden apples.   And the houses are so hand-
some ! For vastitude and for amazing antiquity, even
the holy and beautiful house at Jerusalem yields to those
temples.   And then, this glorious river ! With balm
above, and reflecting the spotless blue, it seems to carry
in solution all the ages which have wandered by its
brink, and all the shadows which have dropped into its
tide—sphinxes, pyramids, palaces.   And as the lotus
lifts its chalice to the light, whilst the crocodile lurks
below ; as from its far-off source it suddenly arrives, with
bounty in its bosom and sunshine on its face, but with a
dark secret in its heart, and then holds on its way, most
ancient of rivers and most mysterious,—at once an
emblem of human life, an epitome of human history,—we
know the fascination it exerts on many a pilgrim of our
modern time.   Like a liquid spell, a floating poem—as
you surrender to its sorcery, your inch of duration
expands into epochs, and into your own life you take up
the thousands of years preserved in these changeless

monuments. Aching nerves soothed, chafed lungs com-
forted, it feels as if every furlong that you float bore you
farther and farther from all that is dangerous in disease
and from all that is painful in the past. And with sen-
sations so novel,—with existence made so easy,—you
not only forget your father's house and your own people,
but you forget the frailty of your frame. In self-
complacent catholicity you become tolerant of strange
customs and strange creeds ; and it is well if, amid the
pleasant witchery, you remember the deceitfulness of sin,
and retain in sharp demarcation the rules and restrictions
of the Decalogue.

Even had the wanderer been a man of faith and
fixed principle, there are temptations in travel ; and away
from wonted influences and restraints, it needs special
watchfulness and prayer,—it needs the special grace of
God,—to keep the way of holiness. In his Egyptian
journey even the faith of Abraham faltered ; and
although his pious errand may protect the evangelist,
and his grave pursuit may be some help to the explorer
or the trader, novel scenes and foreign ways are a great
trial to the tourist. His errand is relaxation, amusement,
unbending ; and in order to bring back a clear con-
science and a purer piety, as well as health and spirits,
he would need to remember everywhere, " Thou, God,
seest me." And after all, of the traveller's reminiscences
the most delightful are Bethel and the seaside at Troas,
spots consecrated by the communion of saints and fellow-

ship in prayer—made memorable by the nearness of Heaven and glimpses of the glory of God; or places like the road from Jerusalem to Gaza, or the river-side at Philippi, where strangers were drifted together, and a passage of Scripture was read, or a conversation ensued, which made it on either side an interview much to be remembered.

Our traveller, unfortunately, had no good errand. He merely wanted to enjoy life and see the world, and be sufficiently far from home. And we have fancied him come down into Egypt. Notwithstanding its cruel treatment of his ancestors, this country was still attractive to the Jew, and it sufficiently meets the requirements of the parable. Beautified by the Greek and enriched by the Roman, the old colossal Egypt of the Pharaohs had ceased to be formidable, and many a Hebrew found his way to such a city as Alexandria,—the merchant to make his fortune, the scholar to study in its matchless library, the spendthrift to command its luxuries and enjoy its pleasures.

In the mood of our adventurer, a city of this description was sure to be fatal. In the countryside where he grew up, if there was wickedness, it carried its own warning. The sot was notorious and was shunned; there was no field for sharpers and swindlers; if there had been detected any open sepulchre, with his evil communication corrupting the atmosphere, the nuisance would have been quickly ejected from the neighbourhood,—the scurrilous foul-mouthed scoundrel would have been cast forth from all decent company; and by stamping vice with the brand of villany, society not only vindicated God's law, but preserved itself from many snares and sorrows.

Here, however, it is all so different. Everything is elegant, and at first it is enjoyment sufficient to view the mighty piles of masonry,—the obelisks and colonnades, the public walks and fountains; and as he visits the bazaars, brilliant with the manufactures of three continents, or goes down to the wharf where bee-laden barges and floating granaries are coming in, the bustle and the Babel noises are a stirring contrast to the stupid life at home. Presently, however, the eye is satisfied with seeing, and in quest of refreshment he steps in where food and wine are sold. Prepossessed by the size of his girdle, a stranger enters into conversation with him. The stranger is very gentlemanly, and he must be wonderfully accomplished; for he can speak Hebrew as well as Greek and the native *patois*. Nothing can be more affable; and although his entire air is distinguished—so distinguished that his fine clothes, contrasting with a country suit, bring the blush into our young friend's face, and make him feel like a bumpkin and a boor—he condescends, when asked, to share the flask of wine, and enters with kindest interest into the affairs of the new-comer. The result is an agreeable acquaintance, who undertakes to show him something of the town, and who introduces him to a nice set of friends. They welcome to their society the simpleton with his store of silver pieces. They see that he is, according to our vulgar vocabulary, very "fast" and very "green." Fond of display, they flatter him, and feast at his expense right royally; and not disinclined to dissipation, they lead him on to all evil, even as he is able to bear it; till taverns and theatres, music halls and midnight orgies, are his familiar resort, and in the excess of riot he outruns his tamer or more cautious companions.

We said when principle is weak the "far country" is fatal. It was the loss of this young runaway that he had now arrived where there were few restraints on evil, fewer helps to religion : no Sabbath, no public worship, no stated reading of the Word of God. Even though there might be many of his compatriots in the place, he did not seek them out. He had no wish to fall in with them ; he rather studied to keep out of their way; and so, as long as money lasted and comrades cheered, with equanimity unruffled and conscience unaroused, he kept up the revel, waxing wilder and wilder, worse and worse.

If any one is obliged to leave home—not from love of idleness, not from love of liberty, not from love of pleasure—but on such business as to our large towns brings young men every day—on virtuous errands and with honourable aspirations—willing to work their own way and lighten the load of others—do not forget that God is here. It would be true if you were the only occupant of earth : it is no less true of you as a unit in the million-

peopled city: "O Lord, thou knowest my downsitting
and mine uprising; thou understandest my thought afar
off; thou compasseth my path and my lying down, and art
acquainted with all my ways." But in order that you
may be in the fear of God all the day long, you must
avoid those whose frivolity dissipates thought, as well as
those whose evil courses make it their interest to forget
God's presence or deny His power. Seek out for your
companions the high-toned, the pure-minded, the Christian;
and if occasionally sighing for "the calm retreat, the
silent shade," remember what a holy life was lived by
Daniel in Babylon; remember that at Rome, in Rome's
worst days, there were found friends of Jesus, and in the
palace of the worst of emperors—"saints in Cæsar's
household." Remember, too, that a thing does not be-
come right when it ceases to be repulsive. No doubt
that was a snare to the prodigal. In the far country vice
was disguised as much as possible, and looked quite
another thing in the garb of fashion. So if over their
greasy cards you chanced to see a set of low ruffians quar-
relling—the fiend in every face and blasphemy on every
tongue—you might recall what your grandmother used to
say about the devil's books, and almost vow that you
would never touch them. But go into the Kur-Saal at
Homburg or Baden—a palace in the midst of a garden—
and in glittering saloons with magnificent music, for which
you pay nothing, see Satan enthroned as an angel of
light. They are ladies and gentlemen all: every move-

ment soft and silken, and nothing to interrupt the well-bred silence, except the ivory ball revolving, and the chink of gold and silver, as happy winners garner their harvest of napoleons or florins. Surely amidst these mountains of money there is enough for all, and if it was very wrong the people could not look so respectable. Yet, after all, it is only the tuneful Lorelei seeking to draw down into her gloomy gulf the simple voyager. These tranquil countenances and soft movements are but a masque, a veil, a curtain; and behind—within—as any one can tell who has been there, are bankruptcy and suicide, fraud, peculation, forgery—deserted wives and children cast upon the world—magnificent domains brought to the hammer—and ever and anon a murder. So in our large cities there is a sort of gambling which does not look particularly repulsive; for it is not carried on in "hells," and it pleads the sanction of some titled names; and yet its results are hanging like a millstone round the neck of many a once promising young man, and, to say nothing of those whom it has reduced to beggary or blackguardism, numbers of its victims must be sought in the Portland hulks or Dartmoor prison. They went to the race-course, or, without going there, they laid wagers on horses, and sooner or later they lost more than they could pay, and in dread of dishonour they took means to get the money at the very suggestion of which, once upon a time, they would indignantly have exclaimed, "Is thy servant a dog?" and after a few miserable make-shifts, only adding sin to sin, there came detection, and ruin, and disgrace. Reader, you will be a wise and happy man if you resolve in the strength of God never to lay a wager, and never to play for money. If you would keep the devil at arm's length you will never enter a billiard-room, and the betting-book is a record in which your name will never appear.

The time of a young man's arrival in London is a time of trial; but those who have the prudence or the principle to resist the temptations of the outset are usually preserved to the end.

On a wintry day in 1803 a lad left his native Kelso so sad at heart that, as he stood that night on the bridge at Berwick, the tear had almost frozen on his cheek. It was his eighteenth birthday when he found himself for the first time in our great labyrinth, and on one of the first evenings after his arrival a youth, who from the same vicinity had gone up to town the previous year, took him out to see the sights. The stroll ended in a sort of blind alley, and as his companion knocked at a door it was opened by some light-looking girls evidently well acquainted with their visitor. With instant revulsion the new-comer started back, for instinctively he felt that it was "the house which inclineth unto death." In much agitation he exclaimed, "O ——, where are you going?" and he entreated his companion to come away. That companion only laughed and went in, and as our friend sought his way back to his lodging he felt very desolate. It was a cold and dreary night, and in his disheartened mood he thought that London must be a devouring monster which swallowed up whatever came into it, and changed it into the likeness of its own deformity. Here in a few months it had made a virtuous youth a profligate, and as if walking amidst snares and pitfalls and strange mysteries of iniquity, he trembled for himself. The whole thing was too painful for him, till he went into the sanctuary. But next Sabbath he inquired his way to Swallow Street. There he found the worship which he had learned to love beyond the Border, and as he listened to the earnest sermon he began to feel, " God is in this place." The little church brightened into a Bethel, and helped to cheer the following week ; and then came an introduction to the minister, and a class in the Sunday-school, and the acquisition of one good friend after another ; till at last the streets which at his first arrival were haunted by gloomy phantoms and cruel ghosts, grew populous with brethren in the Lord : till he who had himself been so graciously preserved became distinguished for his efforts in preserving and strengthening younger brethren.

It was on the fiftieth anniversary of that eventful day that our venerable friend, his heart overflowing with gratitude to God, told us this incident. By that time he was an honoured citizen, and his name well known throughout the churches. Numbers of ministers and missionaries knew him. Many widows and orphans knew him. Nearly all our religious societies and benevolent institutions knew James Nisbet.

Under God, that trying evening was the pivot on which turned the whole of his following history.   If he had for a moment yielded—if through curiosity or weakness he had accompanied his guide across the sinful threshold, he might have shared the same fate, and in a few months, with ruined health and morals, been, like him, sent back to his native place a shattered dying invalid.   And unfeignedly do we congratulate all to whom God and a careful up-bringing have given the same blessed and self-protecting purity. It is a pearl of great price ; may it never be flawed or sullied ! And you to whom life in the city is new, pray to God to " turn away your eyes from beholding vanity," and may He enable you to follow their shining track who through the same scenes passed undefiled, and who now walk with Christ in white among the worthy !

You too, kind friends, to whom God has given a pleasant habitation, extend its shelter to the young and inexperienced.   There are some who make a system of this, and many who in various professions are now treading the paths of righteousness look back with gratitude to those whose timely thoughtfulness invited them to the family pew, or on the Lord's day evening offered them the hospitalities of a Christian home.   It is a labour of love which almost any head of a household can render. It were a fitting acknowledgment to Him who, when the path was slippery, upheld yourself; and few efforts are more like the Saviour Himself than the endeavour to strengthen weak principle and protect endangered virtue. It is by fostering the smoking flax that Christ has created all the lights of the world.

Returning to the prodigal : the portion of goods which fell to him must have been a handsome patrimony, and it would have been his wisdom to wait for it till the proper time. In that case, before entering on the actual possession, he would have known how to guide it. He would have learned how to make it more by trading, and he would have learned some temperance and self-control. But with indecent haste he forestalled his reversion, and what he obtained so easily he quickly fooled away. No trinket or toy could he see but his fingers itched till he owned it, and though it had only been in costly jewels and fashionable attire, a short period would have disposed of it all. But then there was the riotous living. The daily bread costs little; but dainties are dear, and are never so costly as when they are gifts from the devil. His comrades treated him, and in return he must needs treat them; and if over exquisite viands and the vintages of distant lands the time flew fast, the money flew faster : till all of a sudden the horse-leeches dropped off, the parasites disappeared; the victim was exhausted, his "substance" was gone.

RIOTOUS LIVING.

E

" The younger son . . . took his journey into a far country, and there wasted his substance with riotous living."—LUKE xv. 13.

THE YOUNGER SON . . . . . TOOK HIS JOURNEY INTO A FAR COUNTRY,
AND THERE WASTED HIS SUBSTANCE WITH RIOTOUS LIVING.

RIOTOUS LIVING.

NOTHING can be nobler than a true and thorough man-
hood, where, amid the seductions of sense, the soul still
retains the mastery of itself by retaining its loyalty to
God. Such men are always impressive : men like Blake,
content with the softest plank for a pillow ; men like
Havelock, who, never thinking of comfort, never lost
sight of duty; men like Grimshaw, who, with meat to eat
that others knew not, would dine on a crust of bread,
then preaching the love of Jesus till the tears ploughed
white channels in the grimy faces of the Yorkshire colliers,
would turn into his hay-loft and find it Eden in his dreams ;
men like Milton, of maidenly purity of heart and heroic
grandeur of purpose, "himself a true poem, that is, a
composition of the best and honourablest things," and
flowing forth accordingly in the stately song which still
ennobles English literature ; men like Paul, who, "keep-
ing the body under, and bringing it into subjection," was
enabled to bring myriads in subjection to the Saviour,
and perform those prodigies of daring and devotion at
which the world will wonder evermore.

Such men command our homage. For the moment

we forget that they are of like passions with ourselves, and they give us a new and exalted conception of what human nature can perform when sustained by high motive and animated by the Spirit of God.

On the other hand, it is deeply distressing to find the higher nature dethroned or in thraldom. Wild stories circulate in many lands. In Northern Europe they tell how a child has been carried off by wolves, and brought up amongst them—taught to live in wolfish fashion, sleeping in the forest, joining in the hunt of the reindeer or aurochs, and drinking with savage delight the blood of the palpitating prey. And in Africa the like story is told —how the man has been kidnapped by the baboon, and, hurried up the mountain, has spent amidst these hideous monsters a horrible captivity.

The risk is real. The climate may be good, the settlement may promise all that heart can wish, and the vicinity may be so far cleared as to make the immediate homestead tolerably secure; but it is folly to deny all danger. A wise man will be cautious; and if cautious he need not be nervous. It is only right and kind to give warning; and pleasant as is the lot of your inheritance, it is well to remember that the thickets and steep places are haunted. Frightful ogres frequent them, and they are sure to sally forth on the heedless wanderer. There are even instances on record where they have vaulted over the enclosure and carried off from the threshold some hapless victim. The names of three of the best known and most mischievous are—the Lust of the Eye, the Lust of the Flesh, and the Pride of Life ; or, as they are sometimes called, Vanity, or the Love of Display; Sensuality, or the Love of Low Pleasure ; and the Affectation of Fashion, or the Keeping-up of Appearances.

As long as the younger son remained at home he was comparatively safe ; but the far country was the native land of these monsters. There was no patrol to keep them down, no reward was offered for their destruction, and being thoroughly bold and fearless, they came down into the streets and gardens ; and this poor senseless youth was soon seized hold of and carried captive at their will.

A hateful sight it is to see the man the slave, the brute the master. At first there may be some disgust, some effort to escape, some feeble, impotent resistance ; but too often it ends in the utter degradation of the higher nature and the brutalising of the man. The old fables come true. The voluptuary becomes a satyr ; the sybarite, the toper, and glutton are transmuted into swine.

For a hundred years England has yielded no scholar comparable to Richard Porson. With a memory in which words and things were alike imperishable, and with that marvellous intuition which enabled him to personate any author, Greek or Roman, and in the broken parchment or faded manuscript at once perceive what Æschylus or Tacitus had meant to say, he had

withal a wit which made him welcome at the board of
rich and clever men; and to feed the wit he plied the
wine, till in floods of liquor wit and wisdom both were
drowned, and, the remains of the scholar buried in mere
beastliness, the sot disappeared from society.   For a
hundred years Ireland has yielded no dramatist, no
orator, equal to Richard Brinsley Sheridan; but even for
that brilliant genius, whose versatile talents brought
London to his feet and carried captive the senate, strong
drink was too powerful, and, in place of bouquets and
ribbons, with writs and executions showering around
him, he lay on his desolate couch bankrupt in character
as well as in fortune, and would have been carried off in
his blankets to the debtor's gaol had not the apparitor of
a mightier tribunal stepped in before the sheriff's officer
and claimed the prisoner.   For a hundred years—nay,
through all the years—Scotland has yielded no poet who
could seize the heart of the nation as it was seized by
Robert Burns—master alike of its pathos, humour,
chivalry.   Alas! that pinions capable of such a flight as
" Bruce at Bannockburn" and " Mary in Heaven," should
have come down to get smeared and bird-limed on the
tapster's bough; alas! that from the Cottar's Saturday
evening he should have passed away to the companion-
ship of drunken ploughboys and coarse bullies in their
night-long carousals in low taverns.   But so it was; and,
standing by the untimely grave of the Scottish minstrel,
truth and tenderness can only say—

" What bird in beauty, flight, or song,
   Can with the bard compare,
Who sang as sweet and soar'd as strong
   As ever child of air ?

" Oh ! had he never stoop'd to shame
   Nor lent a charm to vice,
How had Devotion loved to name
   That Bird of Paradise ! "*

Wine is a mocker ; strong drink is raging. Like the skulls which a savage carries at his girdle or sets up on poles in his palace-yard, and tells the traveller what a mighty warrior this or the other was till his axe or arrow laid him low ; so, of all the sins, Intemperance is the one which, reaped from the ranks of British genius, boasts the most crowded row of ghastly trophies. To say nothing of the many sorely wounded, amongst the actually slain it numbers the musician and the artist, the philosopher and the poet, the physician and the lawyer, the statesman, the preacher, the judge. As we hinted already, for the greater part it gains its advantage by beginning so early and in a guise so little formidable. In elfin minuteness it enters the student's parlour or even the school-room dormitory, and the champagne breakfast or the furtive wine-party lays the foundation of a life-long sorrow. Like the spear some ten or twelve fathoms long with which the Vancouver Indian ploughs the river-bed, and the barbed point comes off in the first great

* James Montgomery.

sturgeon which it pierces, the tenacious fibre uncoiling as
he flies : so, paddling over the surface of society, it is with
a long shaft that the demon of Drunkenness explores for
his victims ; but when one of his barbs gets fairly
through the mail it usually fixes and is fast.   The line is
a long one, and will hold for years.   It marks the victim ;
and the first time he rises another dart strikes through
his liver, and then another, and at last a great many :—
the social glass leading on to the glass suggestive or the
glass inspiring, and the glass restorative leading on to
the glass strength-giving, and that again to glasses fast
and frequent,—glasses care-drowning, conscience-coaxing,
grief-dispelling,—till, gasping and dying, the hulk is towed
ashore, and pierced through with many sins, weak, wasted,
worthless, the victim gives up the ghost, leaving in the
tainted air a disastrous memory.

Whether coarse or refined, riot speedily wastes the
reveller's " substance."   Not only does it sap the consti-
tution, and soften the brain, and shatter the nerves, and
enfeeble the mind, but it exhausts the estate, and soon
brings the spendthrift to poverty.   And if the passion
still urge and the fear of God has departed, wild methods
will be tried to meet the demand and assuage the frantic
craving.   Keepsakes will be sold or pledged, to part
with which would once on a time have looked like sacri-
lege.   Money will be borrowed as long as any one will
lend it, and then it will be taken from the till, or inter-
cepted on the way from a customer or correspondent ;

and thus—it is a tale a thousand times told—dissipation leads on to dishonesty; and in keeping up the jovial life, nay, in merely keeping up appearances, character will be vilely cast away.

On a Saturday morning in July 1850 two inquests were held in Newgate. One suicide was a pugilist, who, on the previous day, had been sentenced to die as a murderer; the other was an insurance clerk, who had, on the same day, been adjudged to ten years' penal servitude. His name we need not recal; but it is well to know his story. As a clerk, he had a salary of £200 a-year, but he had tastes for the gratification of which two hundred a-year was a trifle. Fond of the theatre, it became the height of his ambition to be personally acquainted with those glorious creatures who on the stage personate kings and queens, and he was greatly flattered when some of them accepted his invitation, and partook at his expense of a costly supper. The experiment was so successful that it was soon repeated; but in entertaining actors and actresses no actor of them all was sustaining a part so arduous as his own. He was too illiterate to be a judge of plays, but in such cases the want of scholarship is readily forgiven to a wealthy man. And it was for a wealthy man that this patron of the drama needs must pass, and with infinite effort—effort compared with which the tight-rope is pastime—for six years he kept up the illusion. His equipage in Hyde Park so elegant, his suburban villa so splendidly furnished, giving by turns a quiet *déjeuner* or a sumptuous banquet, he was applauded as a fine open-handed fellow, and was envied, as a man is apt to be envied who is made up of money. But when the truth came out and he was proclaimed a swindler and a thief, his poor dastard spirit could not survive the degradation; and after such a taste of luxury, what a prospect ten years of prison fare and servile drudgery! The profligate was caught, but the prodigal did not come to himself; and so from within those gloomy walls, in the same short summer night fled by the same guilty exit spirits twain—the blood-stained murderer, and the man who, by false appearances, and for the praise of fools, had doubly destroyed himself.*

On a winter morning in 1856—a Sunday morning—a friend of ours, a physician, was sent for to the Hampstead work-house. It was to view a lifeless body which had been just picked up in the neighbourhood of a pond, and which there was no difficulty in identifying. A member of Parliament, once a junior Lord of the Treasury, a chairman of banks; able, influential, successful, what could be wanting? what could go wrong? The great wants were integrity, openness, truth: and the thing which put him all wrong was the pride of life, and the consequent need to keep up a hollow appearance. For this he forged documents and issued false shares, and embezzled funds to the extent of hundreds of thou-

* *Facts, Failures, and Frauds*, by D. Morier Evans, pp. 74-105.

sands of pounds ; and when opium could no longer dull
the corrodings of conscience, and the evil day was im-
minent, he wrote to a friend : " Dear Robert,—To what
infamy have I come, step by step, heaping crime upon
crime! and now I find myself the author of numberless
crimes of a diabolical character, and the cause of ruin and
misery to thousands. O how I feel for those on whom
this ruin must fall. I could bear all punishments, but I
could never bear to witness the sufferings of those on
whom I have brought such ruin. It must be better that
I should not live. O that I had never quitted Ireland!
O that I had resisted the first attempts to launch into
speculations! If I had had less talents of a worthless
kind and more firmness, I might have remained as I once
was, honest and truthful, and I would have lived to see
my dear father and mother in their old age. I weep and
weep now, but what can that avail ?" Then putting a
bottle of poison into one pocket and the silver cream-jug
into the other, as soon as the streets were quiet he rose
from his lonely tea-table, and from the warm well-carpeted
room in Gloucester Terrace walked forth into the cold
February midnight. Carrying his load of guilty memories
he climbed the hill to Hampstead Heath, and passing the
darkened houses where, their week's work done, the
honest trader and the day-labourer slept securely, he
sought the spot where the largest and most successful of
swindlers was to lay down the burden of a life no longer
bearable, and add another commentary to the ancient

texts, " The way of transgressors is hard. Happy is the man that feareth alway."

Our hearts are weak, and we have continual need to pray, "Deliver us from evil;" for temptations are sometimes terrible. When in front of his own cathedral Bishop Hooper was fastened to the stake and the fire was slowly burning, they held up a pardon, and told him that he had only to say the word and walk at liberty. "If you love my soul, away with it!" was the exclamation of the martyr as every tortured fibre called for pity, but the loyal spirit revolted from the wicked-ness. So there may come a fiery trial where the ad-versary has got in pledge your income, your earthly prospects, your parents or your children, and asks if you will be so infatuated as to cast them away when the stroke of a pen, the pronouncing of a word, a nod or sign would suffice and save the whole. When the furnace is thus seven-times heated it will need much grace in view of the proffered bribe to cry, "Away with it!" and yet, through His timely succour, who, in the days of His flesh and in view of an awful alternative, poured forth strong crying and tears, such ordeals have been en-countered by men of like passions with ourselves, and from this lesser Gethsemane they have emerged with spirit softened and character confirmed, enriched by the loss, perfected by the suffering.

However, it was not by a roaring lion, but by a plausible tempter that man was first led into evil; and

our greatest danger arises from the subtlety of Satan
and the pleasures of sin.

> " I've heard that poison-sprinkled flowers
>   Are sweeter in perfume
> Than when, untouched by deadly dew,
>   They opened in their bloom.
> I've heard that with the witches' song,
>   Though harsh and rude it be,
> There blends a wild mysterious strain
>   Of weirdest harmony;
> So that the list'ner far away
>   Must needs approach the ring,
> Where, on the savage Lapland moors,
>   The demon chorus sing.
> And I believe the devil's voice
>   Sinks deeper in the ear
> Than any whispers sent from Heaven,
>   However soft and clear."*

Gratuitous wickedness is rare; nor is it by a single
bound or stride that eminence in evil is attained. In
doing wrong the transgressor usually fancies that
there is an absolute necessity : he cannot help himself :
the end justifies the means: and when once the poisoned
perfume is inhaled, when once the "weird harmony" has
beguiled the sense—that is, after the first false step has
been taken—the devil suggests, " In for a penny, in for a
pound. The money will never be missed. Nothing
venture, nothing win." Or in conjunctures more horrible
still, and when there seems only one way to cancel the
debt or conceal the delinquency, he whispers, " Dead

* Aytoun's *Bothwell.*

men tell no tales ;" and now that the last of fifty steps, all wrong, but all seemingly inevitable, has proved a plunge into the abyss, the evildoer wakes up with blood on his hands, with a ghastly crime on his conscience, with the sting of the never-dying worm in his bosom.

If you would pass innocently through a difficult world, keep within the rules. Let your life be open, your eye single, your walk in the broad light of day. If a mistake is committed, lose no time in acknowledging it ; and beware of getting complicated with unprincipled or low-minded companions. They will be sure to use you as the cloak or the catspaw of their own designs, and then, when their purpose is served, or when the day of disclosure arrives, they will sacrifice you and save themselves.

Keep within the homestead. If compelled to quit the parental roof, cast yourself all the rather on your Heavenly Father's grace and guidance. And do not forsake the sanctuary. Many years ago we remember a fine youth who from the far north came up to be a clerk in the Post Office. For a long time he was constant in his attendance on the means of grace, and retained his amiable hopeful dispositions. But by-and-by his visits to the house of God became desultory ; and not only did he disappear from the church, but he became shy of our own society. Years passed without seeing him, and then we were asked to visit him at the Old Bailey. It turned out that he had fallen in with careless acquaintances, who had drawn him away from his earlier friends, and led him to misspend the Sabbath. Eventually he had married a worldly-minded woman, with stylish notions, and in order to supply her expensive tastes he had ended by taking money out of letters. We asked when he had been last in his old place of worship. He said that it was on the Sunday after his first offence had been committed, and when the sermon referred to an agitation then in progress for a Sunday delivery of letters in London. Bearing as it did on the circumstances of his own downfall, he still remembered an expression to the effect :—" The fear of detectives is a poor substitute for the fear of God ; nor will the authorities find it easy to obtain as servants men willing to break the Fourth Commandment, but warranted to keep the other nine." In his case, however, the broken Sabbath was no fault of the authorities. The day of rest was at his own disposal. The departure from God was his own evil heart, and so were the consequent dishonesty and ruin and disgrace.

Keep within your income. As we hinted at the outset, the great temptations to expense are the lust of the eye, the lust of the flesh, and the pride of life ; and to these the great antidote is, not a limited income so much as a large self-denial. It is the lust of the flesh when the little boy spends all his halfpence on sugar-plums. It is the lust of the eye when the peer cannot resist the porcelain of Sevres or the mosaic of Rome, but exhausts his estate in adorning his palace. It is the pride of life when the servant flaunts in finery and lets her parents starve; when the merchant spends on his mansion or his equipage all by which his neighbour or the world might be profited. But just as people can be profuse who are not earning a penny, so there are rich men who do not riot, and who in the generous use of their income enjoy a continual feast. If self-denying, you too will be rich. From personal expenditure saving all that you can, you will find it available for the most blessed of all bestowments; and in paying the school-fees of a younger brother, in a thoughtful gift to a sister, in lightening the burden of a toil-worn father, in promoting the comfort of a faithful old servant who can work no longer, in a subscription to the missionary society or the Sunday-school excursion, in contributing to the happiness or welfare of others you will reap the divine reward of self-denial.

A MIGHTY FAMINE.

F

" And when he had spent all, there arose a mighty famine in that land ; and he began to be in want."—LUKE xv. 14.

HE WENT AND JOINED HIMSELF TO A CITIZEN OF THAT COUNTRY, AND
HE SENT HIM INTO HIS FIELDS TO FEED SWINE.

GOD has given us rules, and guarantees that if we keep them all will go well. These rules are very plain, and it is no small recommendation that they can be understood and carried out by ordinary common-place people.

" Believe on the Lord Jesus Christ, and thou shalt be saved. In all thy ways acknowledge God, and He will direct thy steps. Your heavenly Father will give the Holy Spirit to them that ask Him. Keep thy heart with all diligence. Let no corrupt communication proceed out of your mouth. Let your yea be yea, and your nay be nay. Owe no man anything. Be pitiful, be courteous. To do good and to communicate forget not. Bear one another's burdens. Be thou in the fear of God all the day long. Be careful for nothing ; but in everything, by prayer and supplication, with thanksgiving, let your requests be made known unto God ; and the peace of God, which passeth all understanding, shall keep your heart and mind through Christ Jesus."

There are great differences. There are small natures, and small gospels. There are men whose mind has not much more than one faculty, and whose creed is contained in a single saying; and there are others to whom the whole manifestation of God comes welcome, and who in the sixty-six books of the Bible, and in the long annals of our human history, as well as n the large panorama of creation, recognising the God and Father of our Lord Jesus Christ, in the light of God's countenance pursue their daily task, and fill up with numberless pursuits and experiences an existence all the more comprehensive because it is all redeemed, and all the more susceptible because none of it is remote from God.

However, spring's homely harbinger, with its two notes, sings as sincerely as the nightingale revelling through the diapason; and cheered by that love which is too abundant for the soul of an angel, the most limited nature will be made loyal, obedient, and filial. Such a nature will go by God's rules, and keeping these it cannot miss the way to welfare in either world.

Nay, so good are God's rules, that provided none of the others are transgressed, a single rule faithfully followed will conduct to some delightful or desirable landing-place. "Gather up the fragments that nothing be lost" made the fortune of Laffitte the banker. "Well, old fellow, how did you get together all this tin?" said the brusque youth to the wealthy Quaker. "By one article alone, in which thou also mayest deal if thou pleasest—civility," was the reply. And just as, by adhering to God's rules of frugality and courtesy, these men made

their fortune, so it was, by his possessing a monopoly of
another virtue that Schwartz the missionary saved the
garrison of Tanjore. The soldiers were dying of starva-
tion, but the peasantry would not bring supplies, for they
did not know the Europeans, and could not trust the
rajah; but when the promises to pay were signed by
Schwartz, the rice came pouring in, followed by nearly a
thousand bullocks. In such a case the one pound gains
many pounds, and the single excellence elevates all the
character.

On the other hand, all may be lost by one transgres-
sion. The heart of this young man died away from his
home. That home ceased to be sacred; his Father was
no longer paramount. He felt as if he could do without
either: nay, with his new notions and purposes, he
would rather forget them; so he " took a journey," and
did not stop till he reached " a far country," and found
everything around him strange and novel. The branch
had not only ceased to abide in the vine, but, " cast
forth"—fairly over the wall and out of sight,—it speedily
withered. Grace was gone. Prayer was given up. Good
feelings faded, and now that temptation and combustible
corruption came together, he was soon set on fire of hell.
Lust and passion flamed forth, and he and his substance
were quickly consumed with riotous living.

The home of the branch is the vine: the home of
the heart is God. That, dear reader, is the place for
you. Honour thy Father in heaven. Love the Lord

with all thy soul. Morning by morning go forth in His blessing : and evening by evening, as you return with your finished task, your tribute of love and obedience, in child-like tenderness tell over the faults of the day, its sins and its errors, and for the sake of that dear Son who pleaseth the Father alway, ask and obtain forgiveness.

But if from the tree of redeemed humanity you have cut yourself off—if from that Saviour into whom your " engrafting was signified and sealed" when parental piety placed the lamb in the arms of the Good Shepherd, and prayed that you might be more vitally and more entirely His than theirs—if from that "gentle Jesus, meek and mild," whose hands upheld your first feeble goings, and towards whom you once felt such simple and pure affection, you have now gone away, it is not for us to predict what shall be the first spark to fall into your withered heart; but, dissevered from the Tree of Life, we know too well that you are a brand prepared for the burning. Perchance the fire is already kindled. Lasciviousness, excess of wine, the slow fire of covetousness or the frenzy of gambling, worthless companionships and hollow ostentation, may already have possession of that mind from which ingenuousness, and faith, and loving-kindness, have fled away; but unless God in His mercy snatch the brand from the burning, the soul and its substance are sure to be wasted by this sinful propensity.

In the figurative language of the parable, there arose in the far country " a mighty famine." Extravagance

soon brings the noble to ninepence,* and in the far
country it is not far that ninepence will go. But there
may be so mighty a famine and so great, that even the
noble will not buy the loaf of bread.

One of the most pitiful incidents in the history of
British genius is the death of Chatterton. We by no
means quote it as a case of riotous living; but it will
illustrate the " want" which comes over the spirit when
other resources fail, and the Father's house is far away.—
When a mere boy of seventeen he had passed off, in
the name of an ancient English monk, poems of his own,
with the archaic style so admirably simulated, and the
historical allusions so adroitly managed, that for a time
many clever men were taken in, and surmised no forgery.
Elated by the success of this imposture, and conscious of
no common powers, from Bristol he came up to London.
There he promised himself a career of fame and fortune ;
and as he visited the theatres, and watched the grand equi-
pages floating past, he saw in no distant vision the day
when his verses should be in the mouths of men, and
when the doors of the lordliest saloons would open to the
poet. But the fame was slow in coming, and meanwhile

---

* Describing the separation of Mr. Badman and his bad wife, Bunyan
says, " They had sinned all away, and parted as poor as howlets.
And, in reason, how could it be otherwise ? He would have his way, and
she would have hers; he among his companions, and she among hers :
and so they brought their noble to ninepence."—*Life of Mr. Badman*,
chap. xviii. The noble was six shillings and eightpence.

the money failed. Hampered by no restraints of con-
science, he made up his mind to pass himself off for a
surgeon, and get appointed to a ship ; but before he could
carry his unprincipled scheme into execution, he found
himself quite penniless. " Heaven send you the comforts
of Christianity," he wrote to a correspondent ; " I request
them not, for I am no Christian." Bitterly boasting his
disdain of Christianity, and his independence of it, he
fell back on his own resources, and a fortnight after, a
jury brought in a verdict of *felo de se* on a strange self-
willed youth found dead in his little room in Brook
Street, Holborn.

He cared not for " the comforts of Christianity," and
so when the mighty famine arose—when editors no longer
cared for his effusions, and when the frauds and figments
of years began to collapse—with hunger in the cupboard,
and with heartless Muses staring at him so hard and
stony—the trials which in a Christian bring out the
mettle and make the man, in the case of poor Chatterton
left no resource save arsenic and impotent anathemas on
human kind.*

* " Quiet, plain scholars have lived, before now, in German or Scotch
university towns, on boiled peascods for months, or a single guinea a
quarter, earned by teaching, without saying much about it. Had youths
of this type been in Chatterton's place in London, in August 1770, they
would most probably have survived the crisis. They would have
availed themselves gratefully, and yet honestly, of such small immediate
aid as those aunts and others that we hear of so slightly in Chatterton's
letters might perhaps, though poor, have willingly offered at the sharpest

Reverting to the riotous living : not only does it ex-
haust the worldly substance, but by exhausting health and
spirits, it destroys the power of enjoyment. Poor as are
the joys of sense, it is a stupid policy which would distil
into a single cup every pleasure, and in one frantic
moment drain it dry. Where life and reason have survived
the wild experiment, the zest of existence is gone, and
waking up to a flat and colourless world, fastidious and
fretful, blasted and blasé, in a frequent loathing of life
and a general contempt of mankind, the voluptuary carries
to the grave the sins of his youth.

There is an instructive parable, not so much dwelt on
as it ought to be. " When the unclean spirit is gone out
of a man, it* walketh through dry places, seeking rest,
and findeth none. Then it saith, I will return into my
house from whence I came out; and when it is come it
findeth the house empty, swept, and garnished. Then
it goeth and taketh with itself seven other spirits more
wicked than itself; and they enter in, and dwell there ; and
the last state of that man is worse than the first."† And
although primarily pointed against that Jewish " genera-

moment of the emergency ; and, even failing that, they would have con-
quered by sheer patience."—Masson's *Essays, Biographical and Critical,*
p. 316.

* The authorised version has " he," making it appear as if it were
the man, who walked. The original is neuter (ζητοῦν, ἐλθὸν), referring
throughout to the unclean spirit.

† Matt. xii. 43-5. Luke xi. 24-26.

tion," the parable is deep in meaning and is widely applicable.

As has been remarked, " There are the fiend-like and the brute-like sins. The one leads frequently to the other; and the most hideous of all conceivable horrors is that combination of the two in mingled cruelty and lust, of whose possibility many a page of history bears witness. But in their origin, and most commonly in their development, the two are widely apart. There are the sins which men commit under the influence of the animal passions—sins of unchastity, drunkenness, gluttony—and these rob them of their manhood's crown, of moral self-control, and sink them for a time to the level of the brutes ; and there are the sins which men commit under the influence of self-interest, hatred, and all the anti-social passions—sins of cruelty, perfidy, envy—and these do more than sink men to the level of the unmoral brutes ; they degrade them to the likeness of devils. As God is love, so is His antithesis hatred ; and as man rises to the God-like through love, so he falls to the fiend-like by hatred."*

Now it will happen that at some period of life—perhaps quite early—a man is possessed by coarse passion. "Let us eat and drink, for to-morrow we die ; " and he flourishes the wine-cup, and gives himself over to the wildest jollity. But somehow or other he is led to reform.

* " Christian Ethics," extracted from *Theological Review*, Sept. 1864.

His health gives way, or he gets a great fright, and there is a marked change in his habits. It is not that the Spirit of God has come in, but for the present at least the unclean spirit is gone out, and without becoming a Christian, it is so far well that he seems effectually cured of his revelry.

Wearied, however, of wandering in dry places, the old demon returns, and the house is empty. There is no strong principle pre-occupying the heart, no good angel to guard the gate, and, familiar with all the avenues, the foul spirit enters the vacant domain. But this time he is not alone. He has brought with him seven spirits worse than himself. Is it possible? Is he not an " unclean spirit," and can anything be worse than lewdness, debauchery, drunkenness? Yes, indeed. Bad as is the beastly, it can be exceeded by the devilish ; and in order to fathom the lowest depths of abasement, to drunkenness, revelling, and such like, must be added hatred, variance, revenge, misanthropy, murder, and the nature already embruted shall be dragged downward and yet downward by the fiend.

Of this transmutation of the coarse into the cruel—of this eventual merging of the beastly in the diabolical—we have countless examples, and on every scale, from the Herods and Neros of other days down to the Rushes and Palmers of our modern time. Nor is it only the individual who blunts his sensibilities by vice who is likely to end in blood and violence, but the sottish nation soon grows sanguinary. Rome became voluptuous, then shouted for gladiatorial games; and by the unspeakable orgies of the Parc-aux-Cerfs France was prepared for the stream of slaughter which poured for months along the Place Louis Quinze.

Of the two things—the impossibility of appeasing heart-hunger without going home to God, and the danger that the unclean spirit, if not effectually expelled, will introduce others worse than himself—we know not that we can adduce an example more conclusive than Lord Byron.

It was the curse of this gifted man to inherit wealth without the grace to guide it, and so he obeyed the impulse of a strong and wayward nature, and wasted it on wassail. But in the land of Revelry there arose a mighty famine. It was not merely that funds ran short and farms were coming into the market, but there was something in his nature too lofty to be long content with pleasures so poor and low. Like generous wine, we might have hoped that it would rectify itself, and, having thrown down its feculence, would come out mellow, rich, and clear as the purple amethyst; when, alas! the thunder got into it, and turned it all to vinegar.

The sensual was transformed into the malignant. " I have been looking into a dreadful book," says Dr. James Alexander, " Moore's *Life of Byron*—the life of one debauchee written by another. It is the most instructive comment I ever read on the divine word—' The way of transgressors is hard.' Voluptuary as he was, ever sighing after some new pleasure, and drinking to its depth the cup of worldly and sensual enjoyment, Byron seems to have experienced little less than a hell upon earth. Here I read in awful colours the tormenting power of uncontrolled selfishness. Remorse without repentance, and self-contempt without amendment, are dreadful scourges. From country to country he fled, but he carried the scorpions with him. His later works are only a disgorging of tumultuous thoughts and cruel passions—lust, mortified pride, and malignity—as if he would outrage the world even at the expense of every pang in his own bosom. Happy the poorest, weakest sufferer that believes in Christ."*

There is a frightful fiendishness in scattering firebrands, in sowing thistle-down, in systematically spreading contagion and death. But such were the last literary toils of Lord Byron. Before he took leave of society and song, he launched his final venture, and freighted it with blasphemy, impurity, and all sorts of devilry, and then sent it drifting towards his native shore. A poor apology for the wickedness is the poetry. The contagion may be carried about in a goodly garment—the tares, the thistle-down, may be dealt forth from an embroidered bag—the incendiary coals may be scattered from a golden censer; but the propagandist is none the less a miscreant—the crime is none the less a treason against humanity.

* *Thoughts*, by Dr. J. Alexander, p. 420.

Was he happy? Take the last lines he wrote—the lines on his last birthday :—

> " My days are in the yellow leaf;
>   The flowers and fruits of love are gone ;
> The worm, the canker, and the grief,
>   Are mine alone.

> " The fire that on my bosom preys
>   Is lone as some volcanic isle ;
> No torch is kindled at its blaze,
>   A funeral pile !"

Was he happy? On the night before Bellingham was hanged, he went to see the sight. " Seeing an unfortunate woman lying on the steps of a door, with some expression of compassion he offered her a few shillings; but, instead of accepting them, she violently pushed away his hand, and starting up with a yell of laughter, began to mimic the lameness of his gait. He did not utter a word; but," says Mr. Bailey, who tells the story, " I could feel his arm trembling within mine as he left her."* Can any man be happy, who, himself the victim of vile passions, has strewn his path through life with the wrecks of virtue ? who not only carries live coals in his bosom, but those cockatrice eggs which, even here, as they leap into life, and begin to exert their fiery fangs, give terrible presage of coming shame and everlasting contempt ?

No, reader, the Most High has so constituted the

* Moore's *Life of Byron*, 4to, vol. i. p. 357.

mind of man that the indulgence of the malevolent affec-
tions itself is misery; and of all the paths which at life's
outset invite the inexperienced traveller, the surest to
pierce through with many sorrows is the path of sensual
indulgence.   It is a vain attempt

> " With things of earthly sort, with aught but God,
>   With aught but moral excellence, and truth, and love,
>   To fill and satisfy the immortal soul."

But you are not mocked by your Maker.   Those great
and glorious objects exist for which he has given you an
affinity, and towards which, in their most exalted inter-
vals, the highest powers in your nature aspire.   There is
truth, there is goodness, there is God.   There is the life
of Jesus recorded in the Book ; there is the Spirit of God
now working in the world.   Ponder that life till, associ-
ated with a living Redeemer, it shines around your path
a purifying protecting presence.   And pray for that Spirit,
till under his kindly teaching you " taste and see that the
Lord is good"—till expanded affections find an infinite
object—till He who has thus strengthened your heart is
become your portion for ever.

FEEDING SWINE.

G

" And he went and joined himself to a citizen of that country ; and he sent him into his fields to feed swine.   And he would fain have filled his belly with the husks that the swine did eat : and no man gave unto him."—LUKE xv. 15, 16.

HE WOULD FAIN HAVE FILLED HIS BELLY WITH THE HUSKS THAT
THE SWINE DID EAT

FEEDING SWINE.

To how much the portion of goods amounted which the younger son took with him we are not told; nor are we told how long it lasted. But once it is in the hands of a spendthrift, wonderful is the speed with which money disappears. As paragons of senseless profusion Dante has handed down the names of Stricca and his companions,* who sold their estates and bought a princely mansion where they might spend their days in revelry. Their horses' shoes were silver, and, if one came off, the servants were forbidden to pick it up; and, with like disdain of mean economy throughout, the united fortunes lasted only twenty months, and they finished off in the utmost misery. The Sienese spendthrifts have been often distanced in our living day; and the low taverns along the Thames, where our sailors waste their hard-won earnings—the hotels of Melbourne and San Francisco, where successful diggers fool away in a flash of riot the gold for which they have toiled so long, after a coarse and vulgar fashion could parallel the wildest waste of Heliogabalus or Lucullus.

* *Inferno*, canto 29.

More remarkable than the speed with which the
money disappears is the small satisfaction which it yields.
Here, in London, you can order a dinner at from five to
seven guineas a-head, and if there are ten guests their
entertainment will cost you from sixty to eighty pounds.
And everything shall be perfectly quiet and orderly—
no excess, no noise, no revelry; but out of this large
expenditure how much happiness have you created? Of
the company perchance one or two, with a palate ex-
quisitely educated, may appreciate the rare viands and
rarer wines; and one or two more may tell it to the first
acquaintance they meet next morning, subjoining—" But
really I would as soon have dined at home;" and of the
remainder some may regret the waste, or envy the
wealth of the entertainer, or laugh at the vain show.
Suppose that, instead of this feast for your rich neighbours,
you were laying out the money in a treat to the poor; sup-
pose you took a ragged school or the inmates of a work-
house to the seaside or the country—in the previous
chapter we are told, " When thou makest a feast, call the
poor, the maimed, the lame, the blind : and thou shalt be
blessed; for they cannot recompense thee : for thou shalt
be recompensed at the resurrection of the just;"—with-
out even waiting till then, you will find in the pleasures
of the moment an anticipation of the final reward. Your
guests may not make speeches, nor feel all of them exactly
as you would have liked; but they have had a holiday
and a wholesome meal. Away from mephitic dens, they

have inhaled pure oxygen; eyes dull with looking at grey
pavements and dusty yards have been refreshed with
green fields, or have sparkled at the boundless blue, and
when their hearts were filled with food and gladness,
words have been spoken, hymns have been sung, which
helped to make them love God and their fellow-creatures
more. The day will be a bright spot in a hundred memo-
ries, and a protracted feast to the giver of the festival.

From wasteful expenditure small satisfaction remains;
but if, like the prodigal, your expenditure be on self-
indulgence and excess, the more money the greater the
misery. If you had stood on the bridge and dropped
the sovereign straight down into the river, it would not
have come back into your hand any more than the
sovereign spent at the play with a jolly supper after-
wards; but it would not have left a pain in your head,
and a self-loathing in your spirit. If, like George Heriot
with the king's acknowledgment, you had put the bank-
notes on the hearth, and sent them flaming up the
chimney, they would have left you far richer than those
you have spent on reckless companions and riotous living.
If, like Cleopatra, you had dissolved a pearl—if you had
put together the income of years—all that has been spent
on self-indulgence—perhaps in enticing others into sin—
could you have put it all together, and, like the queenly
jewel, dissipated it in dust and air, we might have been
sorry for the idle sacrifice, but the wasted money would
not have wasted you. Cleopatra had another pearl, the

gift of peerless beauty. That gift was perverted, and it hatched a serpent; it came back into her bosom—the asp which stung her. So with the possessions of the prodigal. Talents laid up in a napkin, pearls melted in vinegar, will benefit no one; but rank, fortune, health, high spirits, laid out in the service of sin, are scorpion-eggs, and fostered and fully grown, the forthcoming furies will seize on the conscience, and with stings of fire will torment it evermore.

Whatsoever was the fortune which our spendthrift took into the far country, it was now exhausted. He knew what it was to come to the last shekel, and eat the last dry crust. He knew what it was to saunter along the street, and look wistfully in at doors and windows, and pass on with the painful knowledge that his pocket was empty. And it was astonishing how quickly his old companions found out his altered circumstances. Some who had lately feasted at his cost were seized with sudden blindness, and could not recognise him; and others, who used to have loads of leisure, were now in a perpetual hurry, and could only wave a flying " How do ?" as they hastened past. And it might not be all hard-heartedness; for they were beginning to be badly off themselves. There had arisen a mighty famine, and whilst the poor were perishing, those not absolutely destitute were reduced to inferior fare and short allow-ance. Already—the last coin vanished—the prodigal had converted everything into bread : rings, chains, orna-

ments of every kind; and as, owing to the hard times,
the market was glutted with such trinkets, it was little he
obtained : and now, with a best robe or dress-coat in a
bundle, or some such relic of his recent finery, he might
be seen stealing up back alleys, or bashfully entering
some dingy shop and asking a small advance from
the hawk-faced owner ; till money, ornaments, apparel,
everything, was eaten up, and still the wolf kept howling
—still he felt as if he must perish with hunger. In des-
peration he threw himself on a wealthy citizen. Oh, how
unlike his own kind father, this proud and surly pagan !
and how unlike his own dainty fastidious self, this
willingness to dig—this eagerness for drudgery ! But
anything to keep soul and body together : bid me do
anything so as I may earn a morsel of food. " There,
Moses, there are the hogs : go, feed the swine." Oh,
yes ; he will : his spirit is broken ; there is no pride now.
Utterly abject, unable to resent the bitter mockery which
assigned such employment to a Jew, and amidst the un-
clean creatures feeling the isolation of the outcast, the
self-contempt of the apostate and renegade, he drives
forth to the field his loathsome charge.* But though

---

* Remembering what Herodotus says as to the Egyptian detestation
of swine and swineherds (ii. 47), the reader may think that there is an
incongruity in making Egypt the scene of the prodigal's sojourn ; but
these animals figure on the remaining monuments of old Egypt, and
the herdsman or driver as well, with his whip and his noose, as repro-
duced in the picture of Mr. Selous (see Wilkinson's *Manners and
Customs of Ancient Egypt*, vol. iii. p. 34) ; and Herodotus himself

there is food for the swine, there is none for him. The
day is far spent, and his fast is not broken. No meal
is brought out; no menial comes near him. It is plain
he is forgotten; most likely on purpose. But these
crooked pods, which the pigs are so greedily crunching,
do not look so bad, and he has seen them in the hands
of the children and beggars. He tries them, but alas!
so husky and hollow, they only mock his hunger. Faint
and weary, for an instant he closes his eyes, and in his
dream, behold, he eateth! but he awaketh, and his soul
hath appetite. The landscape is a skeleton. Vegetation
droops; the earth is iron; and, sickly and swooning,
nature seems as if about to give up the ghost. It is the
Far Country, and the Far Country in Famine.

Whether it be a natural nobleness, or an acquired
refinement—the one, the direct gift of God; the other,
an indirect creation of the gospel—it is seldom forfeited
all at once. Step by step the downward path is trodden.
The heart dies away from God. The prodigal goes forth
from His presence; and, love being lost, fear soon fol-

---

assigns a use for them: if not permissible as food, they still were
serviceable to the husbandman by treading the seed-corn into the soil
left soft by the refluent river. The "husks" on which they were fed are
the crooked, horn-like pods of the carob-tree, *Ceratonia siliqua.* It still
grows abundantly in Egypt and the Holy Land. See "Husk" in Fair-
bairn's *Imperial Bible Dictionary.* The lover of Shakspere will re-
member Orlando, "Shall I keep your hogs and eat husks with them?
What prodigal portion have I spent that I should come to such penury?"
As You Like It, act i. scene 1.

lows. He does that which is good in his own eyes—
works the will of the flesh and of the mind, and seeks
his happiness in riotous living—in those forms of self-
gratification which suit his temperament, whether that
be animal or intellectual, coarse or æsthetic. Then
comes a period of exhaustion and depression. The
substance is wasted. Money and credit are gone, and
the power of enjoyment is gone. Nerves are shattered,
life is vapid, the old sensations pall. There is a famine
in that land; and, in despair, he tries the husks which
the swine do eat. He flies to fierce excitement and
strong stimulants—betting, gambling, speculating, drink-
ing; or, utterly demoralised, he becomes a bold beggar,
fastening himself on any acquaintance or stranger who
does not forcibly shake him off, glorying in his shame,
amongst villanous associates boasting his good con-
nections or his former respectability, and, snatching
tit-bits from the swine-trough, shows how thorough is the
transformation since he fell from his first estate.

In the days of the Regency there was a man much
envied, and in the ranks of fashion his influence was para-
mount. It was not that he was a statesman or a hero, a
thinker or a speaker; but, as far as an outside can make
it, he was the gentleman. His bow, his gait, his dress,
were perfection : the Regent took lessons at his toilette;
when peeresses brought out their daughters, they
awaited with anxiety his verdict, and no party was dis-
tinguished from which he withheld his presence. Very

poor padding within, heartless and soulless, the usual saw-
dust which does for a dandy, by infinite painstaking and
equal impudence he scrambled into his much-envied
ascendancy, the arbiter of taste, the dictator of the draw-
ing-room, the leader of the great army of beaux and
butterflies. Then came a cloud. The prince withdrew
his favour, and, of course, the prince's friends. His
mysterious wealth suddenly took wing, and means which
he took to recover it sent him into life-long exile at
Calais and Caen. He had no God.* His god was the
sunshine—court-favour, the smiles of the great and the
gay. The instant these were withdrawn, the poor Apollo

---

* A more godless existence than poor Beau Brummell's it is im-
possible to conceive. The ideas of accountability and worship do not
occur, as far as we remember, in all the conversations and letters
preserved in the two volumes of his biography. Even as consul at
Caen he never so much as paid the mark of respect to the religion of
his country implied in a visit to the English place of worship, and the
chaplain, who often visited him in his last days, writes :—" He appeared
quite incapable of conversing on religious subjects. . . . I never,
in the course of my attendance upon the sick, aged, and dying, came in
contact with so painful an exhibition of human vanity and apparent
ignorance and thoughtlessness of and respecting a future state ; for I
have before visited persons whose mental powers were equally shattered,
but still it was possible to touch some chord connected with religion,
to which they responded, though perhaps weakly and imperfectly :
with him there was some response when sounded on worldly subjects,
none on religious, until a few hours before he died, when, in reply to
my repeated entreaties, that he would try and pray, he said, ' I do try,'
but he added something which made me doubt whether he understood
me."—Jesse's *Life of George Brummell*, vol. ii. p. 350.

butterfly came fluttering down, down into the dust, and never soared again. It was all in vain that old acquaintances tried to keep him out of debt and discredit. With no gratitude, and with little conscience, and with only that amount of pride which makes the misanthrope, he begged and borrowed on all sides, at the *table d'hôte* glad to get a bottle of wine from some casual tourist by telling stories of old times, and unable to cross the threshold when his only suit of clothes was in process of repair. The broken-down exquisite began to be in want, and, when borrowing a biscuit from a grocer, or a cup of coffee from a kindly hostess, he may have remembered the days when he lavished thousands on folly, the days when he was the favourite guest at the palace. Truly, it was a mighty famine, but it did not bring him to himself. It only alienated from mankind a heart which had all along been estranged from the living God, and gave frightful force to his cynicism. " Madame de St. Ursain," as he said to his landlady, " were I to see a man and a dog drowning together in the same pond, and no one was looking on, I would prefer saving the dog."

Just to take one instance more where the portion of goods was vilely cast away. More than fifty years ago, in the pleasant town of Tiverton, there was a clergyman, popular and clever, but by far too fond of field-sports. One day, however, a friend, a mighty hunter like himself, suddenly expired whilst uttering most impious language. The awe-struck minister abjured dogs and guns, and begging his people's prayers, vowed to live henceforward for his sacred calling. For months his preaching was earnest and impressive, but at the end of that time he resumed the sporting life with fresh devotion, and over and above betrayed a passion from which few are delivered. He had acquired a love for gaming. A presentation to Kew-cum-Petersham brought him to the neighbourhood of London, and gave him opportunity to frequent the gambling saloons of St. James's; and whilst numbers were reading with delight his *Many Things in Few Words*, poor " Lacon " himself was sitting far into the night among swindlers and pigeons, and then slinking home to a suburban hovel to sleep as best he could till far into the day. The upshot was, that he was forced to abscond, his living was declared void, and after leading a vagabond life between New York and Paris, the clergyman, the author, and the late fellow of King's, perished by his own hand at Fontainebleau.*

And whether it be Richard Savage, whose riotous living at last imbrued his hands in another's blood, and then landing him in the debtor's prison, left him to be buried at the cost of the kind-hearted gaoler; or Emma, Lady Hamilton, passing like a meteor through foreign courts, and making wise men mad with brilliancy and beauty, then cast off by society, and from a sordid lodging

---

* In 1832. There is a brief notice of Caleb Colton in Rose's *Biographical Dictionary*, and some interesting details are given by a fellow-townsman in the *Leisure Hour* for 1855, p. 42.

carried in a deal box to a nameless grave; or men like
Beckford, who, spending prodigious wealth in self-idolatry,
have lived to find that the idol was not worth the wor-
ship;—by cases which it would weary you to quote, we
might show how invariably, if there be but time to work
out the legitimate sequel, separation from God ends in
desolation and sorrow. We might show how often the
wayward child, who would not sit contented at the Father's
board and eat the children's bread, has ended at the stye
and been fain to clutch at husks which the swine do eat.
And from the nature of the case, as well as the Word
of God, we might show how inevitably the far country
becomes a waste and howling wilderness, and how, soon
or late, the soul which there abides must die of hunger.

But we weary you. You would rather hear something
on the other side, and to that other side we gladly turn.
And if self-seeking can never be successful—if separation
from God is the death of the soul—if carelessness about
others' welfare, not to say misanthropy, is misery, there can
be little difficulty in deciding what is life and joy and peace.

Love to Christ is happiness. Our late friend David
Sandeman was naturally of a sombre temperament; but
when it pleased God to reveal to him the Saviour, it was
a total transformation. It almost lifted him off the earth,
and made him hold so lightly house and lands, and even
dear kindred, that he was saved, what is to some of us
a sore distraction, a divided heart. The night when
he was dying of cholera at Amoy a friend asked him,

" Have you any pain ?" and he answered, " The only pain
I have known since I knew Jesus Christ is *sin.*"   " Have
you any message to your friends ?"   " Tell them, it was
only last night that the love of Jesus came rushing into
my soul like the waves of the sea ; so that I had to cry,
Stop, Lord, it is enough.   O the height, and depth, and
length, and breadth, of the love of Jesus ! and I was con-
strained to cry out—

> 'All too long have we been parted ;
> Let my spirit speed to his.'"

Christ did not disappoint him.   For His name's sake he
had sought that far country, and very pleasant did he
find the Master's service there.   But the task was soon
ended, and death was swallowed up in victory.

Harmony with God is happiness.   You may feel, " I
am not capable of such concentration.   Mine is not a
fervid or rapturous nature.   It must be very blessed to
feel like Sandeman, or rather to feel like Paul—For me
to live is Christ.   But with dispersive tastes and a desul-
tory turn—fond of books, fond of friends, fond of travel
—I despair of being ever drawn up to that height of de-
votion where One Object is the only spectacle, and love
to Him the only feeling."   But if love to Christ is the main-
spring of Christianity, Christianity itself is the completion
or renovation of our manhood—the emancipation from
sin's dominion of the human nature—the " new " but
original " creature " set free for the service of God and
for the enjoyment of all God-given happiness.   Hear the

testimony of one who for the best part of fourscore years had lived this life: " I have heard some say that ' worlds should not tempt them back to tread again life's dreary waste.' Such language is not for me. I should not shrink from the proposal of repetition. ' Goodness and mercy have followed me all the days of my life.' My duties have not been burdening and irksome. My trials have been few compared with my comforts. My pleasures have been cheap and simple, and therefore very numerous. I have enjoyed without satiety the seasons and the sceneries of nature. I have relished the bounties of providence, using them with moderation and thankfulness. I have delighted in the means of grace ; unutterable have been my delights in studying and perusing the Scriptures. How have I verified the words of Young—

'Retire and read thy Bible to be gay !'

I have seldom been without hearing of some instance of usefulness from the pulpit or the press . . . I have a better opinion of mankind than I had when I began my public life."* Compare the dissenting minister with Beau Brummell—the one taking God's way of it, the other always taking his own :—the fop always scrambling after costly enjoyments, and finding them apples of Sodom in his grasp ; the contented Christian avowing, " My pleasures have been very numerous, for they were cheap and simple ;" the self-centred exquisite leading a life of perpetual

* *Autobiography of the Rev. W. Jay*, p. 158.

envy and vindictiveness and spleen,—the unambitious and cheerful man of God radiating on others his own bright, devout, and hopeful feelings, and so ending with an improved opinion of mankind, whilst the disappointed worldling finished off by saying that rather than save a man he would rescue a drowning dog.

To dwell on high is happiness. You may think Mr. Jay might well be cheerful, for he was healthy and active and free from all ailment. Hear then what Dr. Arnold says of his sister, long the victim of hopeless disease : " I never saw a more perfect instance of the spirit of power and of love, and of a sound mind; intense love, almost to the annihilation of selfishness—a daily martyrdom for twenty years, during which she adhered to her early-formed resolution of never talking about herself; thoughtful about the very pins and ribands of my wife's dress, about the making of a doll's cap for a child,—but of herself, save only as regarded her ripening in all goodness, wholly thoughtless ; enjoying everything lovely, graceful, beautiful, high-minded, whether in God's works or man's, with the keenest relish; inheriting the earth to the very fulness of the promise, though never leaving her crib, nor changing her posture ; and preserved through the very valley of the shadow of death from all fear or impatience, or from every cloud of impaired reason, which might mar the beauty of Christ's Spirit's glorious work." *

* *Life of Dr. Arnold*, letter 52, vol. i. p. 332.

A WISE RESOLUTION.

H

" And when he came to himself, he said, How many hired servants of my father's have bread enough and to spare, and I perish with hunger! I will arise and go to my father, and will say unto him, Father, I have sinned against heaven and before thee, and am no more worthy to be called thy son : make me as one of thy hired servants. And he arose, and came to his father."—LUKE xv. 17-20.

WHEN HE WAS YET A GREAT WAY OFF, HIS FATHER SAW HIM.

A WISE RESOLUTION.

To many a clever man God says " Thou fool!" He says
it to the man who says " No God !"—who, with no father
for his spirit, is content with an ape for his ancestor; or
who, "corrupt and vile," has so embruted that spirit as
to lose all memorial of his Maker, the echo in his con-
science as well as the image on his soul. He says it to
those who, forgetful of the great power of God, doubt if
a resurrection be possible, or who, conceding the fact,
show a needless solicitude as to the method, and, with
officious anxiety, offer Infinite Wisdom their best advice.
And He says it to those whose brilliant husbandry
bursting their barns, they are forced to build greater;
whilst in all their architecture they take no thought for
eternal habitations, and spend neither skill nor effort on
those harvests which alone God receives to His garner.
And in many a history it is the first hopeful moment
when a man says it to himself. That grey morning when
David shouted from the hill-top, and held up the pitcher
and spear which he had carried off from the pillow of his
sleeping persecutor, a gleam of good-feeling flitted over
the spirit of Saul, and he exclaimed, " Return, my son

David : for I will no more do thee harm.   Behold, I
have played the fool, and have erred exceedingly."   In
confessing himself a fool, it almost looked as if Saul were
becoming wise; and although the moody cloud soon
returned and gathered in again, these flickering revivals
of a better time leave a touching pathos round a tragedy
otherwise so severe and sombre.

We have now reached a new stage in the history.
Up to this time the prodigal had no quarrel with himself,
and had never questioned the wisdom of his own pro-
cedure.   He had exhibited forethought and shrewd cal-
culation in the steps he took when leaving home.   Instead
of a penniless impulsive elopement, he had curbed his
impatience, and by securing his portion of goods he had
provided for future enjoyment.   And for anything we
know, amongst his loose companions he may have been
aught but a dolt or a dullard : "a fellow of infinite jest,
and most excellent fancy."   Nevertheless to a sound
mind something more is needful than mere wit, sparkle,
brilliancy, and for true wisdom a poor substitute is
worldly knowing.   This the prodigal began to feel.
Excitement at an end, the portion of goods exhausted,
swine for his companions, a churl for his master,—those
stern realities, hunger, hardship, nakedness, brought him
to himself, and to himself he said " Thou fool ! "

Where there is any nobleness in the nature, it
occasionally happens that the very excess of riot leads to
a revulsion.   " I was converted by six weeks' debauchery,"

says a somewhat paradoxical character in fiction ; and
when the good minister remonstrates against his speaking
thus lightly of the Divine operations, he replies, " I am
not speaking lightly. If I had not seen that I was
making a hog of myself very fast, and that pig-wash, even
if I could get plenty of it, was a poor sort of thing, I
should never have looked life fairly in the face to see
what was to be done with it." *   And when the Spirit of
God enkindles or keeps smouldering on from better days
any of the finer feelings, in the very sight of the swine-
trough there is enough to sober and startle.   Greek
writers tell of a creature which combined every element
of hideousness, and was capable of much mischief as well ;
but if by any chance it got a glimpse of itself, the face in
the mirror was fatal—the sight of the monster slew the
miscreant.   The perfection of ugliness is evil, and if, like
the basilisk, the sinner could only view his own deformity,
it is a sight which self-complacency could never survive.
We have known actual instances, and you may have
known them : instances where there was a long course of
levity and self-indulgence, but no remonstrance was
effectual, till some crime was committed, and awakening
all the furies, conscience shouted in a voice of thunder :
instances where the heart was not given to God, but the
life was so decorous that respectability said, " Thank
heaven, I am not as other men !" till a fall into open
sin killed the Pharisee, and extorted the cry, " God be

* *Felix Holt*, vol. i. p. 111.

merciful to me a sinner :" instances where no warning, no entreaty availed, till in sight of the swine-trough and its wallowing frequenters, the husks dropped from the hand of the prodigal, and he said, " I will arise and go to my father."

In bringing sinners to their right mind, the sobering influence which God most frequently employs is affliction. " Because they rebelled against the Word of God, and contemned the counsel of the Most High : therefore he brought down their heart with labour ; they fell down and there was none to help. Then they cried unto the Lord in their trouble, and He saved them out of their distresses." This history is repeated in almost every prodigal. The counsel of the Most High is contemned, the Father's house is forsaken ; and for a time the sinner is allowed to fill himself with the fruit of his own devices. At first that fruit is pleasant—" fruit to be desired to make one wise,"—opening up new experiences, revealing new enjoyments : the golden apple, the magical mandragora, the Hesperian lotus, gloriously forgetful of home, of honour, and of duty; the Noachian clustre suffusing life with false glamour, and with the lie of the first forbidden fruit cajoling its victim, till the delusion dissipates, till the drunken hero wakes up in the pig-stye, till he to whose last consciousness sounded the whisper, "Thou art a god!" aroused by a box on the ear, sees scowling over him his terrible taskmaster—his demi-god comrades transfigured into hogs, and his own fingers, lately bejewelled and daintily uplifting the goblet, in their gaunt grimy grasp no longer retentive of even such husks as the swine do eat.

If you have been forgetting God, or forsaking the Father's house, the heart which prosperity hardens may be brought down by affliction; and you may well be thankful for the sorrow which sends you home. A man who had a praying wife was himself a drunkard. He was a gambler, and went to all the races within his reach, usually returning tipsy. Fond of fighting, he was withal a brutal husband, and often struck his wife. Beyond all this, as he wished that there was no God, he tried to persuade himself that there is none. There never was a bolder blasphemer. One night, when he was swearing dreadfully, his wife begged him to desist. "Tom," she said, "the Lord will strike you dead." "Who is the Lord?" he shouted, and then started off in oath after oath with the wildest imprecations, defying the Lord to touch him, vociferating and gesticulating till the perspiration stood upon his brow, and he sank down exhausted by his paroxysm of frantic impiety. For capturing a leviathan like this, you would have thought of an iron cable; you would have been for putting a tremendous hook in his nose. But the Lord had hold of him already. How? Through his excellent wife, you reply. Well, she lost her 'father, and on the Sabbath after the funeral she prevailed on her husband to accompany her to church. The sermon was on the depravity of man. He gnashed his teeth as he heard it, and with all his own corruption stirred to fury he turned on his poor helpmate as she came home, and, in her new mourning, kicked her down stairs. But a silken cord, if it be God's, will draw out leviathan—nay, with such a cord in the hand of a little child He can lead the lion. This brutal father had a daughter two years of age, and out of the mouth of this babe the Lord often stilled the enemy and avenger. When coming home in a savage humour, and knocking about his helpless partner, the little Maria would scramble into her mother's lap, and with her pinafore wiping the tears, would gently bid her "Don't cry, mamma," and turning on him a reproving face, would say, "Ah! naughty papa, to make poor mamma cry." This little one he really loved, and this little one the Lord took. Soon after returning from her grave, the father was once more persuaded to enter a place of worship; and this time the word of the Lord found him. The parable of "The wise and foolish virgins" opened his eyes, and feeling that if he continued in his wickedness he must perish eternally, with all the earnestness of an awakened conscience he began to seek salvation. Night and day he sought it, often with crying and tears; and when at last the Saviour stood revealed before him, he consecrated life to His service, and has ever since proved a faithful follower and a valiant soldier of the Lord Jesus Christ.*

True, there are some whom the Lord brings to Him-

* *A Brand plucked from the Burning* (1856). The author is now (1866) a zealous and useful clergyman of the Church of England.

self in ways of wondrous gentleness; like the late saintly Cæsar Malan, whose account of his conversion was, " My heavenly Father awakened me with a kiss." But usually, where there have been great godlessness and reckless- ness, the "riot" is followed by a "mighty famine," and it is amidst the consternation of a sore calamity, or in the wilderness of affliction, that divine mercy overtakes and brings home the wanderer. Towards the close of last century, one of the most gifted men in the Netherlands was a young physician at Dort; but to his Dutch industry he added French philosophy, and with his scientific resources and his energetic self-reliant genius, he dis- carded Christianity and felt no need for God. One day, however, in the capsizing of a boat, there sank into the weltering river his wife and only child, and in that over- whelming moment, poetry and philosophy could do no more to comfort him, than the poor frightened ousel which flitted to and fro shrieking over the scene. The blackness of darkness engulfed him, but through the same chasm at which the flood rushed in and drowned his world there burst upon his spirit the claims of God, the guilt of the transgressor, the need of a Saviour; till after many a dismal day the rainbow of the covenant spanned the flood, and proclaimed the divine forgiveness. Very different from the experience of the gentle Genevese was the struggle towards the cross of this sturdy Hollander. After he had become a missionary to the Hottentots, Vander- kemp's account of it was, " The Lord sprang upon me like a warrior, and felled me to the earth by one stroke of his arm."

Peradventure these pages may be turned over by some one whose life has hitherto been a course of self-pleasing, but to whom the days have come when he says, " I have no pleasure in them." You once were happy, you at least were gay; but you have lost your fortune, you have lost your popularity or your good position; you have lost that large fund of hilarity and animal exuberance which made up for every other lack; or sadder still, there has been taken away with a stroke the desire of your eyes, and now that the light of your life is extinguished, small is the joy which passing hours bring, faint the hope which the future awakens.

Yet, dear friend, if you are wise, from this very season may date the best and most blessed time in all your history. Like the passengers through the tunnelled Alp, from the dark and the cold and the stifling air emerging on the broad light-flooded plains of Lombardy, it is by a way which they know not, gloomy and underground, that the convoy is carried which God's Spirit is bringing to the wealthy place; and your present grief you will have no reason to regret if it introduce you to God's friendship, and to joys which do not perish in the using. It may not have struck you, but you have been trying to create your own Eden, and it was an Eden with the living God left out. For a time the experiment seemed to prosper, but if it is blighted you have no right to complain; and though

it should never blossom again, even the howling wilder-
ness does you a service if it makes you a pilgrim and
turns your face to the better land. Affliction is God's
message. This mighty famine is no accident, it is God's
voice sounding through the far country, and saying to you,
COME HOME !

Yes, at this moment you are miserable. Disappointed
with yourself, dissatisfied with your lot, in broken health,
bereft of your dearest friend, you are in the position in
which sooner or later every one will find himself who has
placed his happiness in things created or things external.
But even at this moment there are many outwardly less
favoured than you who are contented and cheerful.
You are invited to join them. Will you not go ? It
is " bread " you need. You have fasted long, and your
soul is weak : the word of God will give you strength
and stamina. It is clothing you need. If not outwardly
tattered, the inner man is in rags ; God will clothe you
with the robe of a Redeemer's righteousness, and will
adorn you with the garments of the great salvation. It
is shelter you need ; you will find it in the Father's house.
It is honourable employment you need ; you will find it
in the Father's service. It is love you need ; you will
find it in the Father's arms.

Prodigal son ! prodigal daughter ! has not God been
very kind to you ? Is there a good thing you possess
which has not come from His hand ? Is it not in Him that
you have lived and moved and had your being ? Who

was it that through the eyes of your mother smiled over your cradle, and surrounded life's outset with love and endearment? Who was it that for your first tottering steps spangled the turf with the daisies of spring, and fanned your fresh face with its breezes? Who was it that in hushed and holy hours went on before you, through Sabbaths and hymns and Jesus' sweet name, alluring you to glory, honour, and immortality? and whose bright countenance was that which sometimes came so near your own, leaving a soft and pleasant glow, till one provocation after another rose up and darkened all the atmosphere and shut it out for ever? Oh, what a sin to go away from such goodness! what a sin to spend in self-pleasing the gifts of such bounty! what a sin to be a lover of pleasure rather than the lover of God!

Are you not sorry? In forsaking such a home and coming to this far country, have you not played the fool and erred exceedingly? In the life you have led, in the passions you have indulged, in the thorough estrangement of your heart from Infinite Excellence, do you not feel that you have sinned against heaven, and that you are no more worthy to be called God's child?

And will you not arise and go to your Father? Is it not wonderful that He should still desire your return? In His house there is bread and to spare, and He invites you home. Arise and go.

Sobered by his altered circumstances, the prodigal was brought to his right mind, and in the way in which

he spoke of himself and his father he showed right feel-
ing, and in the determination " I will arise and go to my
father," he came to a right resolution ; but the whole was
crowned and completed by his taking the right step : "he
arose and to his father he came." Instead of musing any
longer, he started up and at once commenced his journey.
Disgusted with the far country, its swine and its citizens,
its harlots and riotous living, he instantly and for ever
renounced them ; and his heart full of shame and contri-
tion and a timid tender hopefulness, he had already com-
menced his journey.

That promptitude saved him. If the kind Spirit of
God now moves you, let no pretext detain you ; but
breaking away from every snare, in this propitious
moment and with full purpose of heart give yourself to
God. No time can be more opportune, and whilst God
waits to be gracious all that the devil asks is delay.

A good many winters ago we were sent for to see an
elderly man, far gone in his last sickness. He was in a
wretched comfortless attic near Lincoln's Inn, but had
once been an Edinburgh advocate. He told us his story.
He had been engaged to an accomplished young lady.
Her brother, a dashing officer in the army, and given to
gambling, wanted some one to be his security for £2000.
" It was always my misfortune," said the invalid, " to be
of a soft and yielding nature, and I at last consented.
The money was not forthcoming, neither could I pay it.
As a ruined man, I could not lift up my head in the

Parliament House, and the lady to whom I hoped to be married broke off the engagement, and I never saw her again. After spending some time in the country in a moping melancholy way, I came to London nearly thirty years ago." Then after mentioning how, through the late Mr. Lockhart, he had obtained literary employment, amongst other things publishing a romance, and for a considerable time editing a magazine, in these latter years he had been engaged on a long-projected dictionary. of the Bible : " for although I had no real religion, I wished to have it. I had a good mother, and I had seen pious people in my youth, and I hoped that by being always engaged about the Bible, I might, some time or other, be brought under its saving influence. I spent six years compiling that dictionary, and it was quite a labour of love : but I cannot say that it answered the more important purpose ; for in the literary part of my task I got so absorbed as to have no time for the spiritual." The manuscript, however, was lost. " I was paralysed. At sixty years I could not begin again. The sun of my existence had gone down, and neither object was accomplished. I was not to be allowed to publish a book which I thought readers of the Bible would welcome, and I had failed to find for myself the pearl of great price. I seemed like one bewitched. In order to earn a crust of bread, I have sat down on a summer's morning, intending to write a story for the magazines, and I have folded the paper and dipped the pen and held it in my fingers till it dried; and I have dipped it again, hoping that the thought would come, and gone on in this way till the sun went down, without ever marking the paper. Then I grew so weak that I could not come up these stairs except on my hands and feet, and by-and-by I could not come up at all : and for the last three weeks I have not left this bed, and now they tell me I am dying." Then he burst into tears as he told how he had often come to our own and other churches, and been "almost persuaded" to close with Christ; but he did not tell what had hindered. From other sources we learned that there were besetting sins which kept him back, and from which even for his soul's salvation he could never break away. So there for many years he had stood spell-bound on Balaam's pinnacle, envying the righteous, but never joining their company : a prodigal who knew about the Father's house, but whose "soft and yielding nature" after arising always sat down again; an example of that remissness which lets slip life's long opportunity, perpetually promising that some future day shall be the day of decision, till at last in the shadow of death the last gleam of hope disappears from its eyes.

So you who are still the prodigal, in this lucid interval be entreated, and at once arise. Take leave of every sin : especially in strength of God's own giving flee away from the sin which more easily besets you. And go to God. It is the reign of grace. You are still in the world where pardon may be found. God has not let you go. He has not forgotten you. It is His voice which calls you. It is His Spirit which is striving with your spirit. Notwithstanding all that you have done, He has not yet cast you off for ever. The cord of His love has still hold of you—that cord of compassion, over-strained, ever-lengthening, which you are doing the utmost to sever. Oh, yield at last to God's mercy, and let these bands of love draw you home!

And take with you words. "Father, I have sinned against heaven and before thee. A rebel and a runaway, I am no more worthy to be called thy child. With a heart so depraved, dare I hope that a holy God can have any pleasure in me? and after the life I have led may I look for forgiveness? But with God there is mercy, and although utterly unworthy, I come to thee in the name of that beloved Son who alway pleased the Father, and who came on the Father's behalf to seek and to save that which was lost. I believe the faithful saying. Lord Jesus, who didst come into the world to save sinners, save me. God and Father of our Lord Jesus, magnify the riches of thy grace and the merits of thy dear Son; pity and pardon me. Make me as one of thy hired servants. Weary of wandering, take me into thy house. Weary of self-pleas-ing, let me taste the blessedness of new obedience. Other lords have had dominion over me: henceforth let me be called by Thy name."

A HAPPY MEETING.

" But when he was yet a great way off, his father saw him, and had compassion, and ran, and fell on his neck, and kissed him.   And the son said unto him, Father, I have sinned against heaven, and in thy sight, and am no more worthy to be called thy son.   But the father said to his servants, Bring forth the best robe, and put it on him ; and put a ring on his hand, and shoes on his feet : and bring hither the fatted calf, and kill it ; and let us eat and be merry : for this my son was dead, and is alive again ; he was lost, and is found."—LUKE xv. 20-24.

HIS FATHER RAN, AND FELL ON HIS NECK, AND KISSED HIM.

A HAPPY MEETING.

To the mediation of the Lord Jesus we owe all our hopes and all our happiness. Including, as it does, satisfaction for sin, a matchless exhibition of Divine compassion, and the introduction into our fallen world of that celestial energy which raises to a new and noble life those who were dead in trespasses; it has not only removed every barrier in the way of the transgressor's return, but has made the path of life so open and attractive, that the most simple have found it, the most wayward have been induced to enter, the feeblest have been carried through.

In that mediation so pre-eminent is the work of atonement that in the eye of many a reverent beholder it has left small space for other objects, even as it has left no need for farther manifestations; and with the impatience of gratitude, with the intolerance of an absorbing affection, they denounce, as beside the purpose, all teaching which has not for its theme express and exclusive "Christ crucified."

But right and true as is that sense of sin which nothing can relieve except "the blood of sprinkling," and glorious as shines the cross in the forefront of the gospel, it is no honour to the Lord Jesus, and it is an injury to ourselves, to forget the great lesson of His life, or ignore those other scriptures, without whose light a darkness deeper than was over all the land from the sixth hour even unto the ninth, would still encircle Calvary.

As mediator the Lord Jesus was the manifestation of God. The Divine Son, dwelling in the bosom of Deity, He plainly showed the Father.* Not only did He bring the Father's message, but on the great axiom "I and the Father are One," here in the midst of men He lived out the Father's life, the Father's truth, and tenderness, and love. In Moses the law—the sanctity—had come already, but the graciousness of God came in Jesus Christ;† and in all things like-minded, the very feelings and dispositions of the Father shone in His countenance and breathed in His accents, surrounding His person with a sacred attraction, and with a winsome authority inspiring His words : so that when to the heavy-laden He said, "Come unto me," we know that with like "grace and truth" the Father invites us : so that when on the cross He exclaimed, "Father, forgive," we know that the prayer was addressed not to a Deity distant, inexorable, hostile, but to that God who so loved the world that He gave his Son, and who, in order to answer the prayer in a righteous forgiveness, had surrendered the Bestbeloved to this sorrow.

What, then, is the Divine disposition toward sinners

* 1 Tim. iii. 16 ; Heb. i. 2 ; John i. 18, xiv. 9.   † John i. 17.

here on earth? Assuming God's infinite purity, how far
is He ready to pardon? Acknowledging that there is
but one sacrifice for sins, what is the extent of the Divine
propitiousness? Viewed in the light of the Incarnate
Sufferer, what is the language of the cross? Now that
I would fain break off my sinful life, and give myself to
God, how soon and on what terms may I hope for
acceptance? Must I first prove my sincerity by a long
purgation? or may I come as I am? Must I do some-
thing to mitigate the Divine displeasure? or already
reconciled in His Son, is it so that God actually waits
to be gracious?

To such questions, although not a formal reply, this
parable is an abundant answer.

It was near the close of Christ's ministry, and a
characteristic company had assembled. They were
"publicans and sinners." Attracted by that strange
fascination which drew towards Infinite Purity self-
conscious pollution, many such had by this time sought
out the Saviour;* and by that wonderful word, "Thy sins

---

* "Christ, standing here for us as the representation and revelation
of this Divine love, tells us that whilst it is not caused by us, but comes
from the nature of God, it is not turned away by our sins. 'This man,
if He were a prophet, would have known who and what manner of
woman this is that toucheth Him,' says the unloving and self-righteous
heart, 'for she is a sinner.' Ah! there is nothing more beautiful than
the difference between the thought about sinful creatures which is
natural to a *holy* being, and the thought about sinful creatures which is
natural to a *self-righteous* being. The one is all contempt; the other
all pity."—*Sermons*, by A. Maclaren, p. 33.

be forgiven thee," dissolved into brokenheartedness, and
made to hunger after righteousness, they clung to that
society which promised to fulfil their aspirations.   And
now that before His last journey to Jerusalem a number
of them had once more gathered around Him, the
publicans and sinners drew near, and outside the throng,
separate and self-respecting, stood the Scribes and
Pharisees.   As they surveyed the inner circle, with its
rags, with its disreputable characters, with its wild faces
still carrying signs of former ruffianism, they marvelled ;
and as rapt looks and tear-filled eyes were met by gentle
words and the expansive sunshine of a gratified benefi-
cence, they could not comprehend the manifest affinity
which drew together the Great Teacher and the refuse
of Galilean society : " This man receiveth sinners and
eateth with them."   To meet this natural feeling—for
the feeling must be natural : taken up and passed on
by decent reputable people, the murmur which the Phari-
sees set up has lasted for eighteen hundred years—the
Lord Jesus spake three parables.   They were an argu-
ment from analogy.   As against the feeling of Phari-
saism, they appealed to the instincts of mankind ; and of
the last of the series the purport has thus been given :—

" In my Father's eyes, these sinners, with whom you
say I associate too freely, are not what they are in yours.
You regard them as outcasts ;—He would have them to
be sons.   He looks upon them as lost children whom He
would fain recover to Himself.   His purpose is that I, the

son of his love, should be the first-born among many
brethren. And it is among these sinners that I am to
find my brethren. These sinners, each and all of them,
my Father longs to embrace, as any father worthy of the
name would embrace a long-estranged child coming back
to him again. He has sent me to seek and save them;
—to reveal him to them as a Father, waiting to welcome
them as sons. How think ye? Do I best carry out my
Father's purpose by treating them after the manner you
would have me treat them,—as the offscouring of the
earth,—or by treating them as my Father's children and
my brethren?—so treating them all, including the very
vilest of them—even those who have sunk almost to the
level of the hungry wallowing swine? . . . Thus viewed,
the parable warrants the widest and most unrestricted
proclamation of the fatherhood of God as now, in his Son,
brought within the reach of all,—to be pressed on the
acceptance of all,—with the strongest possible assurance
that all are welcome, freely welcome, to have the full en-
joyment of all that is implied in it, if they will,—when
they will."*

To which we only add that in as far as they are a
disclosure of the Divine disposition towards the sinner,
this and the two companion parables are pervaded by one
principle. There are some seekers—yes, and finders—
who have not first been losers. The merchantman seeks
for goodly pearls, and finds one of transcendent value: the

* Candlish on the *Fatherhood of God*, 2d edition, pp. 199, 200.

farmer seeks for nothing, but sauntering through his field
or upturning the soil, he stumbles on a treasure; and
both are delighted; both are filled with the utmost glee
in this sudden access of fortune. Without ever having
lost, they have found. But here is a shepherd far out in
the desert. Looking anxiously for footprints, listening
for anything like a cry from thorny copse or caverned
vale, brushing the perspiration from his brow, and
when ready to give up roused to fresh effort by a little
flock of wool suspended from that trailing brier : it is of
no use to tell him that he has five score at home quite as
good as the wanderer; nor would you altogether cure his
sorrow though from your own fold you offered the best
equivalent : for this one was his own; he knew it by its
name; it used to go out and in and follow him : and it is
only in the late evening, as you meet him with the weary
truant on his shoulder, that he calls out, "Rejoice with
me : I have found my sheep which was lost." Much the
same with a lost piece of money, still more anxious is
the search for a lost child, and matchless is the joy in his
recovery. When not long ago the three little children
were lost in the Australian wilderness, you remember
how sympathy brought all the neighbours to the search—
how every spot of softer earth, how every tuft of grass,
was questioned for its tale ; and how, without ever count-
ing the cost, or grudging the interruption of their own
affairs, the gallant men could not leave the track as
long as a ray of hope remained. But who can conceive

parental anguish as day after day of that dreary week passed on, and the bread was bitter because they could not share it with their famished offspring away in the hungry scrub, and sleep was terrible, because each new waking revealed the empty cribs or the cold silent sky? And who can paint the rapture as the final night disclosed them nestled under the over-arching broom, beneath the feathers of the Almighty, and the faint " Father!" from the first who waked assured their earthly sire that he had children still?

These are the sentiments and experiences to which the Saviour appeals. To alight on a pearl or piece of money is always agreeable; but if it was one that you had lost, the anxiety of the search gives a peculiar zest to the discovery. If there was joy in the household when it was said, " There is a son born into the world,"—in after years should he be stolen from the threshold, or should he wander away, proportionate to the dismay created by his disappearance and the sorrow with which he has been sought, will be the rapture with which loyal retainership shouts the news of his return and the awful joy with which affection clasps him in its arms. So here, with amazing condescension, Christ represents Himself and the Father as " seeking that which was lost." True, the sheep may have lost itself: the prodigal may have shown vile ingratitude and done very shamefully in going away: but still, to the shepherd it is a grief to lose his sheep; to the parent it is a grief to lose his child; to God

it is a grief to lose the soul made after His own image,
and in which He rejoiced with a Creator's complacency
and more than a parent's tenderness; and because He
is a loser, the Most High becomes a seeker. Into the far
country His love follows the elect soul, and the embrace
of a joyful forgiveness awaits the returning wanderer.

What can be more encouraging? If you have led a
sinful life, and are now ashamed and weary of it, where-
soever else you are welcomed or repulsed, if you arise and
go to God He will receive you graciously and will abun-
dantly pardon. All His assurances are to the same
affecting tenor. "He is long-suffering, not willing that
any should perish." "As I live, saith the Lord God, I
have no pleasure in the death of the wicked, but that the
wicked turn from his way and live. Turn ye, turn ye
from your evil ways." And here He is represented as
the merciful Father whose pity survives the longest pro-
vocation, and whose love is such that when the profligate
at last returns no high-born revulsion hinders, but at once
He presses the tattered swineherd to His bosom. Such
is the God and Father of our Lord Jesus, and if you are
wise you will let no cold suspicions or subtle casuistry
cheat you out of the strong consolation. You cannot err
in believing what the Lord Jesus says; you cannot err in
doing as He directs. Be assured that God "is as kindly
disposed as in this parable He is represented to be. The
calls, invitations, promises which He has given us in the
gospel, mean the utmost of what they express; and God

is as earnestly desirous that sinners should return to Him, and as much pleased when they actually return, as the strongest language of the gospel declares."*

True : God is infinitely holy, and sin is His abhorrence. But the great sin is departure from the living God, and this never ceases till once you return. And if you yourself long to be holy, it is in forgiveness that the fresh start, the new obedience, begins : if you would escape from the bondage of corruption, you must retreat into the home of God and gain the glorious liberty of His children.

True : God is holy, but that will not hinder His receiving you. Holiness means the highest form of all excellence, and every excellence in completest harmony ; and now that, through the satisfaction of the Saviour, there is in the Divine truth and rectitude no obstacle to the justifying of the ungodly, to Holiness itself it is a joy to put away sin and pass by the remnant of transgression. In the condemnation of the offender sin is punished ; but it is only in the salvation of the sinner that sin is destroyed. And as it was in order to destroy the devil's destruction that the Son of God was manifested, in every soul which is restored into the paths of righteousness an incalculable career of wickedness is cut short, and a joy unspeakable is given to that holy Saviour who, in cancelled guilt and arrested evil, sees the travail of His soul. Therefore fear not to make the grand experiment ; cast yourself on the grace of God in Jesus Christ, and you

* Dwight's *Sermons*, vol. i. p. 89.

will find that there is no pity like the compassion of
Infinite Purity. You will find that there is no love like
God's own charity—that love omnipotent which, in saving
a soul from death, not only covers but annihilates the
multitude of sins. And if to a guilty conscience there is
no holdfast so firm as the horns of God's altar, now that
a new and living way has thrown it open, you will find
that for a sin-burdened spirit there is no asylum so kindly,
so secure, so inviting, as the very Holy of Holies.

Therefore we say again : Take with you words, and
return to the Lord. Say exactly what you feel. If you
are not prepared to part with all sin, you are no penitent ;
you are still the prodigal. But if your sin is your sorrow,
let neither past evil nor present imperfection prevent
your return. The younger son was still "a great way
off" when the Father saw him, and was still in his rags
when that Father kissed him. And whilst you cannot
feel too keenly, do not wait for feeling. It is right to be
lowly. To "blush and be confounded" before God, to
"weep and be in bitterness," is no more than the feeling
which guilt should awaken ; and till you have sought and
found forgiveness, you do well to be anxious. As
Bunyan felt after his conscience awoke, when he saw
people much cast down about the loss of wealth or near
relations : "Lord, what ado is here about such little
things ! if they so labour after, and shed so many tears
for the things of this present life, how am I to be be-
moaned, pitied, and prayed for ! My soul is dying, my

soul is damning. Were my soul but in a good condition,
how rich would I esteem myself, though blessed but with
bread and water." No sorrow for the past can be too
poignant; but do not wait for that sorrow. If the pro-
digal had not arisen till he was satisfied with his own
repentance, he would have died in the far country. But
the tears which do not flow from the gaunt eyes of famine,
will come unbidden at the feast of fat things; and the
fountains of the great deep, which freeze in the winter of
remoteness and estrangement, will break up and brim
over in the sunshine of Mercy. The word which you
take, be it what it may, " Father, I have sinned, and am
no more worthy to be called thy son : "

> " Dear Lord, I ask no crown from Thee,
>   No robe with rich perfume ;
> The meanest place will do for me,
>   And in the lowest room :"

"Take away iniquity, and receive me graciously;" what-
soever be the word, let it be a true one, and swifter than
your return will be the footsteps of forthcoming pardon ;
and great as may be your own joy in rescuing and
restoring grace, no less will be the joy in heaven over
your repentance.

The relation which the Most High sustains to his
intelligent and accountable creatures is too comprehensive
and too intimate to be perfectly imaged by any earthly
tie ; but in the relation which runs through this parable

it finds its nearest equivalent.   And what amongst ourselves is fatherhood?   It is that relation which identifies greatness with littleness; which makes it quite natural that the arm which wields the battle-sword should gently rock the sleeping babe; which secures from contempt the master of sentences, the sage, the orator, though he babble idle rhymes in his infant's ear.   It is that relation which lives in the loved one's joy or honour, and which is wounded in his grief or his disgrace; which feels no pride like a son's promotion, and which, gazing at the blood-stained garment, cries, "It is my son's coat! an evil beast hath devoured him; I will go down to him in the grave sorrowing;" but which would rather that the evil beast had devoured him, than that he should live to blight his principles or forfeit a virtuous fame.   It is that relation amongst men which toils and denies itself, and does not grudge the long journeys and the sleepless nights which enable the father to lay up for the children; and both in heaven and earth, it is that relation which delights in being trusted, and which desires to be loved in return; which cannot be asked too many favours, or be entrusted with too many confidences; which seeks one gift only, "My son, give me thine heart," and hears no language more pleasing than, "My Father, thou art the guide of my youth.   Father, forgive my trespasses, and give me this day my daily bread."

Wonderful is parental affection, and wonderful the love of God. "Like as a father pitieth his children, so the

Lord pitieth them that fear him." " Like as a Father;"
but how is that? You see yonder dusky tents along the
stream, and knots of cattle grazing on the neighbouring
hills; but the chieftain stays at home. In the cradle lies
the babe whom a foster-mother is bringing up; for his
own mother died on the day when he was born: and
hand-in-hand with his widowed sire walks a little boy,
full of love, full of notions bright and strange, asking
hard questions, telling dreams: till a sudden change
comes across the scene, and in the effort to be a play-
mate to Rachel's little son, for a moment the patriarch
forgets his cares and griefs, and, as men would say,
his dignity. How is it that a father pitieth his child-
ren? An old king is seated at the city gate. Not
far away a battle is going forward—a battle on which
hangs the monarch's crown, perhaps his very life. And
there is panic through the town—the helpless running to
and fro and the fearful looking forth of those who think
they already see their houses in the flames and red
slaughter rushing through the streets. But now, posting
towards the city, are seen the little clouds—the dust of
separate couriers—and all rush to hear the tidings. "All's
well!" exclaims the first; " Victory!" shouts the second;
but with fierce impatience demands the monarch, "Is
the young man Absalom safe?" and transfixed by the
fatal truth, in his cry of anguish the cheers of exulta-
tion suddenly subside, and as he staggers up to his
solitary chamber, the joyous crowd fall silent, and even

the conquerors, when they at last return, like the per-
petrators of a crime slink through the gate crest-fallen.
How is it that a father pitieth his children? For long
there has been only one son at home, and you might sup-
pose there never had been more than one: all is so com-
plete and orderly, and the new-come servants and the
neighbours never speak of any other. But along the
high-road there is this instant travelling a gaunt and hag-
gard figure; his filthy tattered clothing showing little
trace of bygone foppery, and in his looks not much to be-
token gentle breeding : so shabby and so reprobate, that
those who pity common beggars shake the head or slam
the door on this one. But though the dogs bark at him,
and charity turns away from him; though the meanest
hut rejects him, and though the passengers scowl at his
petitions, one heart awaits him, and keeps for him the
original compartment warm, ample, and unfilled. Yonder,
as he has surmounted the summit of the hill, and is gazing
down on the long-forsaken homestead, and hesitating
whether he may venture nearer, what quick eye is that
which has recognised him a great way off, and what eager
step is this which runs so fast to meet him? and who is
this that in the folds of his kingly mantle hides the rag-
ged wanderer, and clasps him to his bosom, and weeps
upon his neck the tears of enraptured affection, and cuts
short his confession with a call for the best robe and a
command for instant festival? Oh, what a love is that
which the heavenly Father hath unto His children!

THE BEST ROBE.

" But the father said to his servants, Bring forth the best robe, and put it on him ; and put a ring on his hand, and shoes on his feet."—LUKE xv. 22.

,

BRING FORTH THE BEST ROBE AND PUT IT ON HIM; AND PUT A RING
ON HIS HAND, AND SHOES ON HIS FEET.

THE BEST ROBE.

FROM the excellent glory came the voice "This is my beloved Son, in whom I am well pleased; hear ye Him. Obedient to that voice we listen to the Lord Jesus, and we learn the mind of God. We learn His graciousness, His forgivingness, His all-comprehending care and kindness; and taken by the hand we are introduced into His presence, and are taught to say, Abba, Father. Owing to our sinfulness we are very unbelieving, and therefore it takes a long time to learn the lesson; but, encouraged by so kind an intercessor, the experiment is repeated and repeated, till, enriched by faith, awe ripens into filial reverence, and tormenting fear is cast forth by perfect love.*

We obey God when we listen to Jesus; and Jesus says, "Suffer the little children to come unto me : for of such is the kingdom of heaven." If we ourselves have come to love the Saviour, it should be our great effort to endear Him to our children; and the way in which He has taught us to think and feel about God, is the way in which we should try to get them to think and feel towards our Father who is in heaven.

* Matt. xvii. 5, xviii. 22, vi. 9; Gal. iv. 6; 1 John iv. 18.

The very effort will be a great blessing to ourselves.
You who are a Christian parent will acknowledge that of
all your educators your own children have proved the
most influential, and you will allow that to a thoughtful
man the true finishing school is his own family. Even
although a preacher of the word or a doctor of divinity,
you here find the tables turned; and with the watch
which you must set upon your lips, and the faultless con-
duct you are expected to maintain, you find yourself once
more under tutors and governors; the solitary pupil in
the centre of an acute and observant faculty; a scholar
posed by the Gamaliels at your feet; a puzzled Solomon
whose queen of Sheba has just descended from the
nursery with dolls and hard questions. And it is well.
Your turn is too abstract. With you the truths of
Revelation are too much the propositions in a system or
the tenets of a creed: the little child has no turn for
abstractions; to him these doctrines are the sayings of
God, or they are nothing; and rather than live in a pale
ghost-land of dogmas, he will impersonate attributes and
propositions; like the apostle, will clothe in flesh and
blood, Faith, Hope, and Charity; like the Psalmist will
give life to Veracity and Mercy, and be glad to see sun-
dered friends, like Righteousness and Peace, embracing
one another. And it is well to see truth through the limpid
eye of childhood, before the life has gone out, before the
glory has gone off, but just as it comes from God; and
in concert with such unsophisticated students it is good

to open up a text and let out the fragrance and the
sweetness which in the handling of conventional exegetics
are so apt to be sacrificed for the sake of the structural
anatomy.   Above all, it is well to have such an incentive
to personal consistency.   In one sense idealists, children
are also realists ; but nominalists they never are.   They
will not mistake words for things, nor accept profession
in lieu of practice.   You are sometimes forced to say—

> " The man
> Is worthy, but so given to entertain
> Impossible plans of superhuman life.
> He sets his virtues on so raised a shelf,
> He has to mount a stool to get at them ;
> And, meantime, lives on quite the common way,
> With everybody's morals."*

In such transcendental ethics children have no faith, and
the only lesson which impresses them is the one brought
down to their own level—the lesson which is lived.   If
you want them to be truthful, you must never "use light-
ness" yourself, nor make a promise which you have no
intention to fulfil.   If you wish them to be fair and
honourable .in their transactions with one another, the
court of appeal must judge righteous judgment and show
no respect of persons.   If you would like them not to lose
their temper, you must keep your own.   "Walk before
me, and be thou perfect," was God's charge to Abram ;
and "I will walk within my house with a perfect heart,"
was the Psalmist's resolution ; and success in the one

* *Aurora Leigh*, p. 216.

sphere is a good test of sincerity in the other; for next
to the All-seeing Himself, there are no observers so per-
spicacious and so candid as those little ones whom it is
so woful to offend. Let therefore the living God be to
you what you desire and pray that He should be to them :
your fear and your dread, and yet your exceeding joy;
your Guardian and Guide; your Father and Friend.

Wonderful is the teaching of the Holy Spirit. Some-
times prospering parental effort, sometimes with small
outward advantage in the way of example or instruction,
in many an infant mind He has enkindled a sweet and
most natural piety; and although, as too often happens,
blown out in the world's rough weather, so that for suc-
cessive years there is nothing left but the smouldering
wick—the smoking flax of unavailing regret and abortive
resolutions—when the set time comes He has only to
take the begrimed and battered lamp, and pouring in new
oil, with benignant afflatus breathe over it, till, like an
incorruptible seed, the feeble spark, the fiery germ, flame
up a burning and a shining light; whilst other and
happier instances occur, in which the good work has ex-
perienced no marked interruption, but the fair promise of
childhood has strengthened into youthful piety, and manly
decision, and mature devotion : instances like Josiah and
Timothy, like Jeremiah and John the Baptist; instances
like Melancthon, where, early sanctified, the clear intellect
and calm loving heart grew equably together; instances
like John Livingstone, where, never having tasted aught

else than that the Lord is gracious, some experience of
His terrors had to be entreated as a favour; instances
like that described in the touching lines—

> "O God! who wert my childhood's love,
>   My boyhood's pure delight,
> A presence felt the livelong day,
>   A welcome fear at night ;—
>
> I could not sleep unless Thy hand
>   Were underneath my head,
> That I might kiss it, if I lay
>   Wakeful upon my bed.
>
> And quite alone I never felt,—
>   I knew that Thou wert near,
> A silence tingling in the room,
>   A strangely pleasant fear.
>
> With age Thou grewest more divine,
>   More glorious than before ;
> I feared Thee with a deeper fear,
>   Because I loved Thee more." *

Whilst such examples are a great incentive to pious
teachers and parents, the other class may well encourage
those who go forth to the far country and try to reclaim
the prodigal. Even amongst those who have sinned the
worst and sunk the lowest, there are few who cannot
recal a better time, and not a few can recal a good and
hopeful beginning. In one respect yours is a great ad-
vantage. You were not born a heathen. Your child-
hood was not a religious blank, nor was your infant

* F. W. Faber.

imagination filled with hideous pagods; but in "the Lord your Shepherd," in the "gentle Jesus, meek and mild," you looked up and saw a Pity and Protection which it is still touching to remember. Although so sadly fallen, there was once a time when you seemed not far from the kingdom, and degraded though you be, you can still recal a father's house and the beauty of its holiness. At the same time, your case is very critical. Grace resisted, advantages abused, are but a deeper condemnation, and if you die impenitent and unsaved, in the day of judgment it will be more tolerable for pagans than for you.

These latter years have been godless. They have been given to self-seeking and the pursuit of pleasure; in the language of Scripture, they have been spent in "working the will of the flesh and of the mind." But although you have forgotten God, He has not lost sight of you. Even amidst the riotous living His grieving eye has followed you, and the sore destruction, which your sins provoked, long-suffering grace withheld. And now there is in the far country a famine. Health has failed; your post or employment is lost; a dear friend, the desire of your eyes, has been taken away; and amidst the solitary musings of this desolate season, a still small voice keeps passing up and down the chambers of memory, and, in tones not unfamiliar, it recals the happier time. It is the voice of God. It says, "Return, ye backsliding children, and I will heal your backslidings;" and if you are wise you will at once arise and go.

You would fain arise, you say, but you cannot. You are in the arms of a giant. You are in the grasp of a strong and terrible temptation, which holds you fast and will not let you go. You have tried to escape, but it was sure to rush after you like an armed man, and strike you down, and carry you captive once more.

A mournful admission! and yet, if you are in earnest, you need not despair. The kingdom of heaven suffereth violence, and the violent take it by force. When Alfieri's literary ambition was effectually aroused, the great obstacle to progress was a worthless companion. Such was the sorcery of this man's society, that books and vows withstood in vain; and scholarship, patriotism, literary distinction, would have been ignobly forfeited, had it not been for the iron will which a noble incentive supplies. Chained to his desk, at least bound to his chair, and with his hair cropped so as to cut off communion with the fashionable world, he pursued his studies, and in a few weeks the frenzy was thoroughly conquered. Hard was the fight, but it gained the laurel crown. Your aim is higher. More important interests cannot be conceived than those which your present infatuation imperils. Glory, honour, and immortality are now in your offer; God's friendship here, and eternal life hereafter; and of all the wild exchanges which have ever been made since Esau sold the land of promise for a mess of pottage, yours will be the wildest, who for these mean and momentary delights cast away the joys

of a deathless duration. Nor is there any need. For a
hard conflict, a life-or-death struggle, there may possibly
be need; but there is no need for surrender. Stronger
than Satan is the Son of God, and a struggle in His
strength is sure to prevail; and as you would not have
life's remainder degraded, embittered; as you would not
blush to meet that noble army of martyrs who resisted
unto blood, striving against sin; as you would not in a
lost eternity be the derision of devils and the victim of
ceaseless self-upbraidings,—entreat the merciful help of
the Most High, and from this moment forward shun the
path of your destroyer; or should he from cunning
ambush spring on you unawares, cry mightily to God,
who is able to deliver, with a mind made up, that rather
than sin it is good to suffer, it would be gain to die.

Says another, " I have arisen; at least I think I have.
I would fain come to the Father, but I know not the
way. It is now a long time since I first felt anxious
about my state; but although I have never missed my
prayers, and have read the Bible and many good books,
I do not feel as if I had made much progress. I have
no love to God, no enjoyment of religion. I sometimes
despair of ever getting to the Father's house, and I often
feel as if, after all the pains I have taken, I had been only
wandering up and down in the far country."

All that we are told of the prodigal is, " He arose, and
came to his father." We are not told how many days or
weeks were spent on the way home; but in the case of

some it has proved a long and toilsome pilgrimage. From the moment that Augustine arose and left the swine-trough, it was six years before he found himself in the Father's house; and fleeing from the wrath to come, energetic natures like Luther and Bunyan had to fight their path through months of toil and terror, and before they came to peace with God were wearied in the greatness of their way.

In such instances sovereign wisdom overruled for good the sharpness of the ordeal, the tedium of the journey; just as in the long-run it proved all the better for Israel that the fortnight's march from Egypt to Canaan spread out into forty years. But if the traveller is ignorant or wayward—if he has no clear idea of the route, or wastes his time in desultory episodes and refuges of lies—a narrow interval may yield space sufficient for a weary irksome wandering.

And truly it is a narrow interval which divides the Father and the prodigal, the Saviour and the sinner. One day when Joseph Milner, the church historian, was preaching at Ferriby, near Hull, there was present in the audience a man fifty years of age, who had led a life of great and open wickedness. The sermon was from the text, "The hour is coming when all that are in their graves shall hear his voice, and shall come forth; they that have done good unto the resurrection of life, and they that have done evil unto the resurrection of damnation." The conscience of the old profligate was awakened. His life had been spent in doing evil, and at the prospect of the coming judgment he trembled. Of a Saviour he never thought, for he felt that sins like his could never be forgiven; and he could only wish that the race had been extinguished in Noah's flood, so that he himself had never been. Weeks passed in misery. He tried to repent. He tried to soften that hard heart of his; but all in vain: it lay "like a ball of iron" within him. At last he called on the preacher, and as well as he could described his feelings. Mr. Milner listened, and then replied: "We are ambassadors for Christ, as though God did beseech you by us. In Christ's stead we pray you, be ye reconciled to God." He then added: "I now stand in St. Paul's place, and I beg you to believe this invitation. I beg you to accept the pardon of all your sins, which Christ has purchased for you, and which God freely bestows on you for His sake." William Howard stared. "Dear sir, how can I believe that God should invite a sinful wretch like me to be reconciled to him?" and although Mr. Milner pointed out the passage, and explained how God's ways are not as our ways, he was by no means satisfied. He thought Mr. Milner's copy of the Bible could hardly be correct; but when he went home, and in his own Testament read the self-same words, he sank into a sort of swoon of blissful wonder. Here on the one side was a hell-deserving wretch, a horrible transgressor: there on the other was the God of grace opening heaven's door and inviting him to enter. That night was spent in singing the praises of the Saviour who had purchased his pardon, and the holy humble walk of his ten remaining years was another illustration of the truth, "There is forgiveness with thee, that thou mayest be feared."

Said one of our Scottish worthies, "I have seen a great wonder to-day. I found a woman in a state of nature, I saw her in a state of grace, and now she is in a state of glory." Were it given to every one to apprehend as clearly and appropriate as eagerly the blessings within their reach as this poor woman to whose bed-side the steps of the minister were directed, there would be few joyless lives, few tortuous, tiring, self-repeating pilgrimages. "I am the way," says the Lord Jesus. "No man cometh to the Father but by me." As soon as you place yourself in the Saviour's hands, you are practically home. Faith in Christ is peace with God.

Some people once lived in a happy isle, but for their misdeeds were banished. The place of their exile, however, lay within sight of their former home. They could look across the channel and discern the beach, with its border of golden sand, and the hills beyond, with their emerald slopes and cool snow-capped summits. Occasionally, too, in the stiller weather, they could hear voices from that land : the shout of happy playmates ; the tinkling tune of browsing flocks, or the mellow peal summoning to welcome worship. Their own was a land of emptiness. From the brackish bog sprouted a few dingy weeds, and the glairy stems, or mallows among the bushes, were the food of the gaunt inhabitants. Few had any desire to leave, or any hope of bettering their condition. One exception we may notice. He was a thoughtful character. With those deep melancholy eyes, which take so much for granted, and which seldom kindle to the fullest—for they have looked the world through and through, and seen an end of all perfection—glimpses of a noble soul could at times be caught, as it climbed to the window of his wan and wistful countenance. Many an eager glance did he direct towards the Blessed Isle. Fain would he reach it. One morning, on waking, it struck him that the opposite coast was unusually near : so low was the tide that perhaps he might ford it, or at all events swim. So down through the swamp and over the dry shingle he posted ; and then across the sad and solid sand, off which the gentle wavelets had folded, right athwart the wet stones and crackling fuci, where tiny streams of laggard water and crustaceans tumbling topsy-turvy in their crawling haste were trying to over-take the ocean : till abruptly met by the rising tide, he found to his dismay that, deep as was the ebb, the channel still was deeper. Disappointed here, he by-and-by bethought him of another plan. Westward of his dwelling the coast-line stretched away in successive cliffs and headlands, till it ended in a lofty promontory, which in its turn seemed to abut against the Happy Isle. Thither he made up his mind that he would take a

pilgrimage. With slopes and swells, zigzags and wind-
ings, it turned out much farther than it looked; and
when at last, foot-sore and staggering, he got to the
summit, instead of a bridge to the Better Land, he found
it a dizzy cliff, with the same relentless ocean weltering
at its base. Baulked in this final effort, he went down
and flung himself on the rocks and wept. It was during
this paroxysm of vexation, that looking up he noticed a
little boat, with whose appearance he was familiar. He
was a little surprised to see it there, for he remembered
that it used to ride exactly opposite his own habitation;
although, belonging to no one in particular, and not
having brought any of the commodities they cared for,
he and the other inhabitants had never paid it much
attention. Having now nothing else to do, he looked at
it eagerly and somewhat wonderingly. It neared him.
It came close up to the rocks where he was seated. It
was a beautiful boat, with snowy sail and golden prow
and a red pennon flying. There was one on board, and
only one. His raiment was white and glistening, and
his features were such as could only have come from the
Happy Isle. "Son of man," he said, "why weepest
thou?" "Because I cannot reach yonder blessed
region." "Couldst thou trust thyself to me?" The
pilgrim looked, first at the little skiff and then at its
benignant pilot, and said, "I can." With that timid Yes,
he stepped on board, and like a sunbeam, so swift, it
bore him away from that dismal coast; and ere he could

believe it, he was a denizen of the Happy Isle, breathing its immortal air; at home amidst its loveliness, and numbered with its citizens.

The happy isle is peace with God; the blessed state which man when sinless occupied. The dreary land is the state of alienation from the living God, in which, with joyless acquiescence, so many are living. And the little skiff—the only means of passing over from the one region to the other—is the atonement, the intercession of Jesus Christ. It is not by the headland of reformation that you will be able to attain the peace which passeth understanding; nor will you be able to ford the channel even when the tide of worldliness and sin runs lowest. Your repentance, your self-amendment, will not suffice; but peace with God is a gift from God, and He who bought it with His blood, in the gospel brings it to your door. Be thankful. You cannot build your own bridge, nor swim the great gulf: be thankful for the transporting medium divinely provided and divinely sent. Be thankful for this ark of salvation and its friendly pilot. That pilot is the true Elder Brother, and to trust yourself to Him is to make the instant transition from the far country to the Father's arms. There, and in His royal resources, you will find amply supplied all which you this moment lack : the robe of a spotless righteousness; the ring which tells of a restored inheritance; and shoes, the badge of freedom, "the preparation of the Gospel of peace," with joyful alacrity winging the feet, and enabling you to walk at liberty.

THE FESTIVAL.

L

" Bring hither the fatted calf, and kill it ; and let us eat, and be merry : for this my son was dead, and is alive again ; he was lost, and is found. And they began to be merry."—LUKE xv. 23, 24.

FOR THIS MY SON WAS DEAD, AND IS ALIVE AGAIN, HE WAS LOST, AND IS FOUND. AND THEY BEGAN TO BE MERRY.

THE FESTIVAL.

No one acquainted with the subject will undervalue the light thrown on the Bible by recent research. But much as these latter days are indebted to the topographer, the linguist, and the antiquary, when we return to the times of our fathers, it is gratifying to observe how seldom competent intelligence and a reverential spirit have missed the sacred meaning. Were you taking, for example, any passage in the Gospels, it is possible that some modern critic may have settled a jot or tittle which hung in doubt a hundred years ago, and modern explorers have elucidated facts in natural science and allusions to Eastern manners which were once obscure; but with such allowance, if from our modern interpreters you go back to Erasmus with his plain straightforward practicalness, or Calvin with his penetrating decisive insight, or Grotius with his rich scholarship and capacious intellect, you will be surprised to find how little that is "profitable for doctrine, for reproof, for correction, for instruction in righteousness," was hid from predecessors as able as ourselves, as studious, and perhaps on the whole as free from prejudice.

Half-way between the Reformation and the present time lived Matthew Henry. In one of the last summers of Queen Anne, and when Addison was writing *Spectators* or *Guardians*, Henry was expounding the parable of the Prodigal Son ;* and we may quote, somewhat condensed, his remarks on this passage. Of course they are quaint and homely. The polished ease of Kensington had not penetrated to the meeting-house in Hackney, and we rather like the kindly humour which animates the trim precision of the Puritan, and gives it an effect like wit. Indeed, as in the kindred instances of Donne and Joseph Hall and Thomas Fuller, we own a relish for that sprightly wisdom which lightens as it indicates the labour of love ; and for the devout sagacity of our expositor we can desire no more appropriate vehicle than his own sententious playfulness.

" He came home in rags, and his father not only clothed but adorned him. He said to the servants, who all attended their master, Bring forth the best robe. The worst old clothes in the house might have served, and had been good enough for him ; but the father calls not for a coat, but for a robe, the garment of princes : the 'first robe'—so it may be read—the robe he wore before he ran

* Henry's exposition of Luke was begun March 1713, and finished on the 10th of July. That day was the Friday on which Addison published the story of a French gentleman, which forms No. 104 of the *Guardian*. The reader need scarcely be reminded that the *Guardian* was a sort of parenthesis in the *Spectator*, which was resumed after the cessation of the former.

his ramble.* Bring hither that robe and put it on him; he shall be ashamed to wear it, and think it ill becomes him, who comes home in such a dirty pickle; but 'put it on him.' And 'put a ring on his hand;' a signet-ring, with the arms of the family, in token of his being owned as a branch of the family. Rich people wore rings, and his father hereby signified that, though he had spent one portion, yet upon his repentance he intended him another. He came home barefoot, his feet perhaps sore with travel, and therefore 'put shoes on his

---

* This is the rendering of the Vulgate, making στολὴν τὴν πρώτην = ἀρχαίαν, the "first" or "former" robe, the robe he used to wear. But as Alford justly says, "This would not be consistent with the former part of the parable, in which he was not turned out with any disgrace, but left as a son and of his own accord." Here the remarks are excellent of Archbishop Trench, whose book, with Greswell's, is for English readers the great repertory of "things new and old" on this and all the parables. After referring to Zech. iii. 4, he proceeds: "These words ('Behold, I have caused thine iniquity to pass from thee') brought to bear on the passage before us, make it, I think, more probable that, by this bringing out of the best robe, and putting it upon him, is especially signified that act of God, which, considered on its negative side, is a release from condemnation, a causing of the sinner's iniquity to pass from him,—on its positive side, is an imputation to him of the merits and righteousness of his Lord" (Isaiah lxi. 10. Trench *On the Parables*, eighth edition, p. 411). "The στολὴ πρώτη denotes the righteousness of God, Rev. iii. 18; vii. 13; xix. 8. The δακτύλιον, the signet-ring, denotes the seal of the Spirit, the testimony that a man belongs to God; the ὑποδήματα (Eph. vi. 15) denotes the power of walking in the way of God. The entertainment made ready points to the δεῖπνον to which the βασιλεία τοῦ Θεοῦ is often compared."—Olshausen (*Clark's Library*), vol. iii. 42.

feet,' to make him easy. He would have thought it sufficient, and been very thankful, if his father had but taken notice of him, and bade him go to the kitchen and get his dinner with the servants; but God doth for those who return to their duty, and cast themselves upon his mercy, abundantly above what they are able to ask or think . . and the fatted calf can never be better bestowed."

The feast which now took place—to use the words of one whose genial wisdom has uttered many things in the spirit and power of Matthew Henry—denotes "the joy of a forgiving God over a forgiven man, and the joy of a forgiven man in a forgiving God." * The one is a gracious revelation, the other is a blessed experience, and each reacts upon the other. To a forth-going affectionate nature it is a joy to be trusted; to a benevolent nature it is a joy to diffuse happiness; to a holy nature it is a joy to create righteousness and arrest evil; and in the case of every soul that is saved such is the joy of God. And whilst over the son who was dead but who now lives again, He lavishes the riches of His grace, responsive to heaven's happiness there is often shed through the believing soul a joy unspeakable, a peace which passeth understanding.

There can be no greater blessedness than his who apprehends the love of God. Mr. Charles of Bala, the founder of adult schools in Wales, and the originator of the Bible Society, was only eighteen when he heard the

* Arnot *On the Parables*, p. 440.

sermon which first disclosed to him the way of life and imparted to his bright and beneficent career the initial impulse. " Ever since that happy day," he says, " I have lived in a new heaven and a new earth. The change which a blind man, who receives his sight, experiences, does not exceed the change which at that time I experienced in my mind. It was then that I was first convinced of the sin of unbelief, or of entertaining narrow, contracted, and hard thoughts of the Almighty. I had such a view of Christ as our High Priest, of his love, compassion, power, and all-sufficiency, as filled my soul with astonishment; with joy unspeakable and full of glory." No doubt there are natures not emotional, and there are others who live in a foggy atmosphere and seldom enjoy a feast of sunshine. Even those to whom, as converts suddenly awakened or prodigals remarkably restored, the transition is most striking, cannot count on a life-time of rapture. From the very Mount of Transfiguration, although it was "good to be there," it was needful to descend; and although the younger son had never in his existence known an evening like this, the music and dancing could not last for ever. Within they were "merry," but already murmurs were heard outside; and even although there had been no disagreeable inmate to propitiate, the morrow would bring homely duties and grave realities, nor could every day conclude with a fatted calf.

There are few, even among Christians, to whom the

whole of life is festival. Still it is a great advantage, if you have a marked and memorable time in your spiritual history: a day of decision, a day when first you owned the claims of Christ, or gave yourself to God: a book, a sermon, a communion, an interview when your heart burned: some happy hour, which has now become a holy memory. Fain would we hope that the perusal of these pages may be made to some reader such a landmark; or should they fall into the hands of any one who is trying to begin the Christian life, may the Holy Spirit speak through them the word in season!

One of the most earnest men whom we have ever known was the late Mr. James of Birmingham. With a frequent feeling that he had not long to live, his sermons were always practical and often solemnly urgent, and when thrown into the society of others he was usually trying to do good. He was greatly honoured. Commencing his ministry with forty communicants, and a congregation of two hundred hearers, he ended with nearly a thousand church-members, and an audience of twice that number. Of his *Anxious Inquirer* half-a-million of copies have been circulated, and the instances cannot be counted of those whom it has led to the Saviour. On the last Sabbath of his life he preached that gospel which it had been the delight of half-a-century to proclaim, and on the Friday following he wrote to Mr. Birrell, forwarding some recollections of Knill the missionary. "During the last week I had a considerable accession of disease, and am

now quite laid aside, so that I look upon it as the
beginning of the end. I think it probable that with
these few notes on dear Knill's life and labours, I shall
lay down my pen, which has written much; would God
it had written better! But while I say this, I am not
without hope—yea, I may add conviction—that it has
written usefully. In some humble degree, I have aimed
at *usefulness* both in my preaching and writing, and God
has, to an amount which utterly astonishes and almost
overwhelms me, given me what I sought. It seems a
daring and almost presumptuous expression, but with a
proper qualification it is a true one—that usefulness is
within the reach of us all. *The man who intensely desires
to be useful, and takes the proper means, will be useful.*
God will not withhold His grace from such desires and
such labours. O my brother, how delightful is it, not-
withstanding the humbling and sorrowful consciousness
of defects and sins, to look back upon a life spent for
Christ. I thank a sovereign God, I am not without
some degree of this." Next morning he was absent from
the body, and death had set his seal on the testimony
that the man is sure to be useful who has the intense
desire, and who takes the proper means.

Usefulness is your desire. God has been very kind
to you. You have not only received a free forgiveness,
but the spirit of adoption. With the ring on your finger
reminding you of your Father's love, you would like to be
engaged in your Father's business; and with the shoes

on your feet, protecting from injury and making rough places smooth, you can go wherever God gives an errand.

What that errand may be, if you wait on the Lord His word and providence will in due time indicate. For men of zeal and energy there is continual need in the Christian ministry; and with openings unprecedented since the apostolic age, for a cheerful warm-hearted worker there is no field like foreign missions. Even within the limits of many a secular vocation there is ample scope for Christian philanthropy. If a merchant, you may befriend a lad of good promise, and find for him a safe and appropriate opening. If a physician, you may not only save precious lives and mitigate a vast amount of human misery, but, treading in the footsteps of the Great Physician, by the word in season you may heal diseases sorer and more disastrous than any which afflict the body. Law itself may do homage to the gospel, and taking up the cause of the oppressed, or mediating betwixt litigious neighbours, you will find, " Blessed is he that considereth the poor ; " " Blessed are the peace-makers." If honestly earned, even gold may be so consecrated as never to become filthy lucre; and as it simmers on the cottage hob or sings in the kettle of the lonely sempstress—as it strikes the thankful key in the widow's heart, or comes out in the festive chorus of the Ragged School, " Oh, that will be joyful, joyful, joyful!" you will be regaled with better music than if you had bought a season ticket at the opera.

Amongst the trees of the wood there is a vast variety : the sturdy oak, the flexile willow ; the solid maple, the graceful ash; the terraced cedar with cones uprising through each grassy-looking lawn of tender leafery, the larch, in lieu of bells, hanging its scarlet blossoms from every pointed arch of its green pagoda; the stiff stout holly disdainful of the breeze, the fidgety aspen all in a flutter at the faintest sigh ; the spacious chestnut enclasping the glebe in its bountiful branches, the strict solemn cypress with every appressed twiglet pointing straight up to heaven. As with the form, so with the bark or the timber : the ebony sinking like stone, the cork on the crest of the billow; the elder so soft and spongy, the box in its firm structure retentive of the finest engraving; the homely deal, the thyine-veneer emulating the spots of the panther or the plumes of the peacock :—beautiful some, but useful all, and not to be interchanged with advantage. An ashen bow would be no better than a yew-tree lance; you do not choose the fir for the prince's table; and even England's oak would make a sorry mast for "some great ammiral."

Through all God's kingdoms we trace the like variety, and still we find it when we rise to the minds of men. There is endless diversity in their nature, and for every form and style abundant use ; and it is best when they are not transposed. Melancthon would have made a poor substitute for Luther; but the absence of Melancthon would have left it a poorer Reformation. Great as

was the invention of the Sunday school, it was not re-
vealed to Bishop Butler, but was reserved for Robert
Raikes ; and yet if the former had not written the
Analogy, it may be doubted if the latter could have
supplied the desideratum.   And although Jeremy Taylor
and John Bunyan had each a fine fancy, the world is now
agreed that if they had changed places, they could have
made it no better : we are quite content with the *Pil-
grim* of the one, and the *Golden Grove* of the other.

Sanguine and non-sympathetic natures insist that
everyone, if he likes, may do the things which they not
only do, but do so easily.   To a man like Lord Thurlow,
coarse and contemptuous of mankind, it must have been
a simple amazement when his kinsman Cowper resigned
the clerkship of the Lords, because he had not courage
to read aloud minutes and petitions ; but, although the
brazen chancellor was a stranger to all trepidation, and it
would have cost him no effort to read his own rhymes
to the peers of Parnassus, it may be questioned if,
even to secure the Great Seal, he could have written
the " Task " or " John Gilpin."   And, although nothing
can be more true than that talents increase by trading,
it is also true that their right investment—the sort of
trade best suited to each merchantman—is indicated by
the natural turn or faculty ; and we shall serve God and
our generation best by turning to account the gift which
He Himself has given.   You who are fond of children,
as most frank true natures are, give yourself to teaching ;

and you who have a fervid forceful spirit, and find that spirit stirred by the state of our godless multitude, go out into the highways and hedges, and compel them to come in. And you who cannot arrest or keep the children's ear, and to whom aught like preaching would be useless martyrdom, seek out some other ministry : consecrate the business talent, and in the savings bank or provident fund, in the committee or council of the church, "rule with diligence." Or go forth and visit. The tired watcher in the sick-room release for a few hours of needful slumber. Take to the bed-rid child some plaything, to the destitute family some comfort. And whether you offer the brief prayer, or read the words of Jesus to the invalid, "show mercy with cheerfulness :" try to do it as if you came and went in Christ's own company, and then, long after you have left, the consolation will remain.

It is thus that by each following out his own line of things the world's best work has been done; and in the free development and loving consecration of gifts, the Church has exhibited a diversity both useful and beautiful. It was thus that, wherever John Macdonald went in perambulating the Highlands, a wave of spiritual influence went with him; and it was thus that, like a Baptist and a beloved disciple combined, George Whitefield startled and melted all England. It is thus that, in our own day, one Christian lady has sought out the prisoner, and another has softened and civilised the neglected navvy, and a third has mended "ragged homes," and a fourth has invented the Bible and Domestic Mission, and a fifth has rallied to the task of nursing— so arduous, yet so angel-like—the refined and well-trained amongst her countrywomen.   And it is thus that in an employment, however commonplace, and in a corner, however inconspicuous, if you take up the task which your hand finds to do, and throw into it the might which God gives, the result will be genuine, solid, enduring. Let each do his own work in his own way, and, as all good work is God's, you will soon see it a more beautiful church and a better world.

To a few God gives a high calling.   Like Gustavus Adolphus, when, at the close of three exhausting campaigns, he listened to the cry of the German Protestants, and began the contest which to him ended at Lützen, to the Fatherland only ended as yesterday: "For me henceforward remains no rest, save the eternal:" they are summoned to a service, peculiar, protracted, exhausting—a service which conscience dare not decline, or from which, when fairly commenced, they can never break away.   But more usually, instead of a single absorbing pursuit, the Christian's calling includes a thousand details. We remember Dr. N. Murray, the famous "Kirwan" of America, mentioning that in his youth he met an old disciple, ninety-one years of age, and in taking leave the venerable pilgrim left with his young friend a charge which he had never forgotten: "Do all the good you

can—to all the people you can—in all the ways you can
—and as long as you can." If that rule were carried out
by each Christian, it would soon change the face of
society. If you, who are the Christian member of the
family, were setting a watch over your lips, and were in
all things wise, gentle, obliging, self-denying, high-toned,
few in the household could withstand the quiet persistent
sermon; and if the Christian households of the land were
as peaceful as they are pure—if the several inmates were
fair-minded, kind-hearted, mutually helpful—if in the
school, the market, the social gathering, the various mem-
bers lived up to the level of their morning and evening
worship—there would soon be poor chance for the
infidel : apologetics might become an obsolete science :
with such a church in every house, the synagogue of
Satan would disappear from the land.

—The feast is ended. The fatted calf is consumed ;
the music and dancing have ceased; and although there
abides a deep calm thankfulness, the mirth and excite-
ment are over. There is no need, however, to tread the
deserted hall, and grow sentimental because the " lights
are fled," and "the garlands dead." You are home ;
you are in the Father's house ; and if you are a good son,
now that it is morning you will be ready to set about the
Father's business. Without waiting for the word express,
you will proceed as if it were actually spoken, " Son, go
work this day in my vineyard." It is from not remember-
ing this that many a younger son is so wretched. You

are idle ; you are useless ; with plenty of lip-homage, you have little filial affection ; you have not that love to your Father which rouses to activity and self-denial ; and, as if it were a mystery or a hardship, you complain that you no longer enjoy the happiness of your first home-coming. After the rich spiritual food you once enjoyed, the fare seems scanty and common. You come to the house of God, but find no feast of fat things, and it even seems as if on your Father's face there were a displeased look—a very decided frown.

Would you know the reason ? There is a divine delicacy in the ways of God. He does not clog His gospel with conditions, nor is the joy of forgiveness dashed by formal stipulations as to future conduct. He would have you be, not a hired servant, but a son—a son whose interest and honour are bound up with His own ; and if you cannot hear the voice of the neglected vine-yard crying to every idler, " Come, work!" He will not vex you by repeating too often, " Son, go !" Neverthe-less, knowing as you do the will of your Father, and merely saying, " I go, sir," without ever stirring a step, can you wonder that He is grieved at His heart ? can you wonder that your consolations are small ? can you wonder if you feel a dulness and depression which you once thought it impossible that you could ever experience at home ?

AN ANGRY BROTHER.

M

"Now his elder son was in the field : and as he came and drew nigh to the house, he heard music and dancing. And he called one of the servants, and asked what these things meant. And he said unto him, Thy brother is come ; and thy father hath killed the fatted calf, because he hath received him safe and sound. And he was angry, and would not go in."—LUKE xv. 25-28.

THY BROTHER IS COME; AND THY FATHER HATH KILLED THE FATTED
CALF, BECAUSE HE HATH RECEIVED HIM SAFE AND SOUND

AN ANGRY BROTHER.

MIRTH within, murmurs without; joy in heaven over sinners repenting, on earth jealousy—even amongst respectable professors of religion decided disapproval: Such are the contrasts here presented.

They had begun to be merry. The fatted calf had disappeared, but the table was still groaning with good things, and still from storehouse and vineyard the eager attendants kept piling the board; whilst every time that it rested on the worn face at his side, and through tears and smiles predicted a happy future, the father's eye glistened, and as the first embrace was repeated again and again, friends and neighbours would look to one another and say, " Is he not happy?"

But in the midst of it all—so loud that, though amidst the clash of the cymbals and the strain of the harp-strings, bounding feet and busy talk were scarcely audible, the discord at once pierced through the melody —in came the noise of altercation from without. When the prodigal arrived, the elder brother had been "in the field"—at another farm, or on a distant part of the estate;

and it is not a good sign of him that no one volunteered
to go after him and carry the tidings. We suspect
his sullen humour must have been too well known; for
even when he was seen approaching, no one ran forward
in the hope of giving him an agreeable surprise. Accord-
ingly, it was not till he came near enough to notice the
bustle and hear the music and dancing that he demanded,
"What does all this mean?" "Thy brother is come," was
the hearty straightforward answer; "and thy father hath
killed the fatted calf, because he hath received him safe
and sound." To his cold and loveless nature, with its
mean and mercenary spirit, the announcement was gall
and wormwood. What did he care for his brother? a
thorough scapegrace, whose absence was good company!
after all his bad behaviour, how wrong to give him this
reception! And then, as he thought of his own sober life
and steady conduct, his sense of justice was aggrieved,
and he could not curb his indignation. Has it been for
this that the fatted calf was kept? and is this the recom-
pense of long years of service? It was positively unfair:
he did well to be angry. No indeed, he did not want
to go in: he would rather go away. And there he
stood, storming and scolding, till the angry words dis-
turbed the guests and brought out his father.

Who is this elder son? Doubtless, it was intended
that the murmurers then present should recognise in him
their own portrait; just as they should see in this picture
of paternal magnanimity the principle on which, in re-

ceiving publicans and sinners, Christ and His Father
proceeded. "Conceding what you claim—granting that
you Scribes and Pharisees are 'just persons who need
no repentance'—should you not be glad to see sinners
repenting, and wanderers restored to the paths of
righteousness?" But, with its divine and far-reaching
comprehensiveness, the parable suits every case of that
sour self-complacency, which, ignorant of God's law,
thinks it has established a claim on God's justice, and
which, unable to sympathise with divine generosity,
resents as a wrong to itself the kindness extended to
others. It suits the Hebrew Church in the apostolic
age, looking askance at Gentile Christendom, and grudg-
ing that the fatted calf, the portion of Israel, God's first-
born, should be given to the heathen prodigal. It suits
the dry and pedantic professor in a time of religious
awakening, who does not like the excitement and the
interruption of the ordinary tranquil routine, and who
likes least of all the ragged reprobate, the outcast newly
reclaimed, his younger brother. It suits the Pharisee,
who till near the close keeps lurking in almost every
heart. "Who is this elder son?" The question was
once asked in an assembly of ministers at Elberfeldt:
Daniel Krummacher made answer, "I know him very
well: I met him yesterday." "Who is he?" they asked
eagerly, and he replied solemnly, "Myself." He then
explained that on the previous day, hearing that a very
ill-conditioned person had received a very gracious visit-

ation of God's goodness, he had felt not a little envy and
irritation.*

"God's thoughts are not as ours—we gird our breast
    With the cold iron of complacent pride;
Our charities and kindness are comprest
    With earth's hard bands, that check our love's soft tide;
And we to sinners say, with scornful brow,
    'Stand off, for I am holier than thou!'

"Oh! 'tis not thus with God: His arms of love
    Yearn for the thankless prodigal's embrace;
He sees him yet afar, He longs to prove
    His love and pity and forgiving grace:
The Holy Dove spreads soft His peaceful wings,
    And joy in heaven tunes high the seraph's strings." †

Latent in the parable, this brings to light the true
Elder Brother. Shut up and frigid, with no candle of the
Lord shining in his conscience, no coal from the altar
glowing in his heart, the Pharisee has neither the sense
of sin which sympathises with the penitent, nor the loving-
kindness which enters into the joy of a sin-forgiving
God. "Every one that loveth is born of God. He that
loveth not knoweth not God: for God is love." Even
although it had been by nothing else, by His infinite
faculty of love the Lord Jesus proved Himself the
divinest of all men, whilst at the same time He became
to us the most brotherly. With no connivance at evil,
with no compromise of the law's requirement, His was

---

* Stier's *Words of Jesus* (Clark's Lib.) vol. iv. p. 142.
† *Poems*, by the late Mrs. T. D. Crewdson.

that vast compassion which overcomes our evil with its
good—that holy pity which softens into penitence and
helps on to new obedience the heavy-laden transgressor.
Here " in the midst "—here in the gospel of His grace,
and here in His unchanging omnipresence—O sinner, be-
hold your Saviour. It is He who from the Father's
bosom has come to the far country seeking the wanderer.
It is He who assures you that, all provocations notwith-
standing, the heart of God is still fatherly. It is He who
holds out His hand and says to you, wearied of husks and
weak with hunger, " Come, for all things are ready." It
is He who, when you faintly rejoin, "I fain would arise
and go, but I know not the way," makes answer, "I am
the way," and bids you "come boldly." And when you
droop the head and feel that you cannot so much as lift
up your eyes to heaven, it is He who declares that He is
not ashamed to call you brother, and who, Himself giving
the word, bids you say in His name " Our Father."

In the elder son of the parable the frightful feature is
the total lack of affection. Unforgiving towards his
brother, petulant to his father, it turns out that his vaunted
obedience has all along been mercenary, and with his
sulky looks and saucy words he stands before us utterly
unamiable—the impersonation of that darkest, dreariest
thing in all the universe—a loveless self-centered being.

It is a disposition which needs to be guarded against:
for in our fallen nature there are terrible tendencies
towards it. With some it takes the form of a cold cal-

culating selfishness; and just as people who do not want
the swallows to build in their windows take the brush and
coat the corners with oil; so the thorough worldling is
varnished all over. Friends may be useful, but attach-
ments and sympathies are inconvenient, and therefore he
is careful not to permit them. Even his parents, if they
grow old and it is suggested that he might do something
towards promoting their comfort—he is sorry that the
money which might have been otherwise available for
them "is corban"—dedicated to another use, or so
locked up that he cannot get at it. Every appeal to
generosity, to gratitude, to pity, is like the poor martin's
best-tempered mortar applied to the unctuous marble :
met by refusals polite and plausible, from the surface of
a heart fat as grease and hard as stone it falls off ineffec-
tual ; and thus, shutting up his compassions, if there ever
was in him aught like the love of God, it dies away, and
his gloomy soul goes out in the blackness of darkness.
Whilst with others the same sombre spirit assumes a form
more malignant and virulent. With nothing which they
can love—for even their self is to itself unlovable—they
lead the demon's life, and seek a bitter satisfaction in
making others wretched. "Full of envy, murder, debate,
backbiters, haters of God, without natural affection, im-
placable, unmerciful," in the acetous fermentation of their
own perversity the bounties of providence, the assiduities
of kinsfolk and dependants, only sour the temper which
they intended to sweeten; and disdainful of love, yet

indignant at its absence, and for the sake of gratifying a fierce vindictiveness, courting insult, almost glad to be misunderstood or disobeyed, they pass through life fretting and fuming, grumbling and growling, and in their reign of terror give a frightful facsimile of Apollyon's dark dominion.

To be brought into intimate, perhaps life-long relations, with such heartless or malevolent natures, is one of the heaviest crosses which any one can carry. Even simple wrong-headedness is a considerable trial ; and there are in the world a good many "utterly unmanageable persons. You cannot say they are madmen. You cannot say they are idiots. But rationality flickers about them in so strange a way that they are often more difficult to deal with than the utterly irrational."* Yet, perplexing or provoking as such impracticable people may be, and humiliating as are the positions into which their impulsiveness brings us, their folly is often compensated by noble attributes, and the ministering spirit may find the difficult task of guiding and guarding them a labour of love. But alas for the helpmate of a savage ! alas for the child or the servant of a churl ! alas for the human heart on which a swart Vulcan forges his thunderbolts ! alas for the head at which an explosive Jupiter hurls them ! Although even here, in the perfect work of patience and in the maturing of meek and long-suffering graces, there is a certain compensation, and the long

* *Friends in Council*, second series, vol. ii. p. 18.

bondage is usually cheered by fits of rough kindness or gleams of better feeling. But to be "mated to a clown ;" to "radiate affection into a clod :" to waste not merely the wealth of a playful fancy but the riches of a fond and self-devoting spirit on dull irresponsive earthliness, with no compensation in the present, with no hope in the future, this is the sorrow of sorrows. The father in the parable had a son seemingly void of affection, and we have known sons with a father so dreary that they found it difficult to fulfil the fifth command. And who is there over whose spirit there has not flitted a feeling like what Richter has described as his own, riding part of the road with a rustic bridegroom taking home his young bride ?— "Oh, be not so joyful, poor sacrifice ! Thy husband will soon demand of thee neither tenderness nor a light heart, but only rough working fingers, feet never weary, labouring arms, and a silent paralytic tongue." When it comes to that, for heart, for soul, for thoughts which might be accepted if not exchanged, there is no longer any use ; and if they know not to go up to God, the best affections of our nature must just run to waste till the freshness of feeling has exhaled, or till the weariful existence has burned itself away.

All true love is one. The first commandment is very great, but the second is not little. They are upper and nether pools, and the same fountain fills them. He who is richest in the love of God has the greatest advantage for loving his neighbour—for loving his family, his house-

hold, his country, and the world. And that is the best
and happiest state of things—the primal and truly natural
—where, springing from under the throne of God, with a
bright and heaven-reflecting piety love fills the upper
pool; then through the open flower-fringed channel of
filial affection and the domestic charities flows softly till
it again expands in neighbourly kindness and unreserved
philanthropy. The channel may be choked. The de-
votee may close it up in the hope of raising the level in
the first and great reservoir; but by arresting the current
he causes an overflow, and converts into swamp the sur-
rounding garden. In the same way, the materialist or
worldling, content with the lower pool, may fill up the
conduit and declare that he is no longer dependent on the
upper magazine; but from the isolated cistern quickly
evaporates the scanty supply, and thick with slime, welter-
ing with worms, the stagnant residue mocks the thirsty
owner, or as over the bubbling malaria he persists to
linger, it fills his frame with the mortal fever. Cut off
from living water, receiving from on high no consecrating
element, human affection is too sure to end in the disgust
of a disappointed idolatry or the mad despair of a total
bereavement: whilst the mystic theopathy which, in order
to give the whole heart to God, gives none to its fellows,
will soon have no heart at all.

Love is of God, and all true love is one. The piety
which is not humane will soon grow superstitious and
gloomy; in cases like Dominic and Philip the Second

we see that it may soon grow bloodthirsty and cruel : nor, on the other hand, will brotherly love long continue if the love of God is not shed abroad abundantly. And it is as the cradle of either affection—it is in order that life may begin in the sweet union of affection and worship, that God created and in a fallen world perpetuates the home.

To use the words of a thoughtful writer : " God made the first man after a divine original, and after a divine original, too, He made the first home . . . God has not borrowed these images—'father,' 'children,' 'home.' It is heaven that lends to earth, not earth to heaven. The things that are upon earth, the things which have root in humanity as God made it, and which are not the devil's work, are first *there*. Heaven but reclaims its own when it takes these images, and applies them again to heavenly use."* And although the downward tendencies of human nature often make the task tremendous— although the best-intentioned members of the home are after all only sinful beings surrounded by others of like passions and like infirmities—the institution is so holy, and the calling of each member so high, that no effort should be spared, no prayer cease, till it become what God designed and will assuredly help us to make it, a nursery for heaven, by becoming ever nearer and nearer to a heaven on earth.

---

* *The Home Life : in the Light of its Divine Idea.* By J. Baldwin Brown, p. 8.

Dr. Livingstone mentions a place where the people have never seen flowers.* How you pity their children! But on man made after His own image God has bestowed a power corresponding to His own creative faculty; and although—like ants which throw off their wings in becoming workers—most grown people have discarded their imagination before entering on actual life, the little ones still have it; and if there are no flowers, they will quickly make them. If the surrounding atmosphere be warm and genial, wakeful life will be a ceaseless joy: invention will never be exhausted, and the materials of pastime will never be far to seek: a few corks will improvise a navy, and sticks and stones a palace. Only you must keep up the temperature. The fairy-world of the little "makers"—as we used to call the poets—collapses in chill weather, and if, in the shape of a sullen nurse or non-sympathetic mother, a glacier invades the play-room, the frost-bitten Eden is soon replaced by bleak reality, and the expatriated exiles, waking up in an old-people's world, grow joyless and cross, and begin to quarrel with one another.

Very precious is that power which the little children have, and which, when we become as little children, we sometimes get again. It is not entirely creative. There is in it something of the open vision. The cradle of the race was in the midst of beauty, God smiling over it, nature smiling round it; and of a vague blessedness and

* *Missionary Travels*, p. 101.

beauty enough still lingers to make the infant smile back again. When Blake the artist was ten years old he saw at Peckham Rye "a tree full of angels." His father beat and scolded, but young William would not shut his eyes, and all through life kept sight of the angels. And just as "their angels do always behold the face of the Father," so God comes very near them. No check upon their sports, at mention of His name there may be a momentary sedateness, a moment of awed wonder : but still very near, and still notwithstanding all their naughtiness very kind, their faith gives freedom, and the truest reverence is their love. We knew a little girl not three years old. She put into her prayers real desires. One night before lying down, after praying for papa, mama, and her nurse by name, she prayed with the same solemnity for the new kitten. "O God, open little pussy's eyes, and make its tail grow." She was not told that this was wrong, or bidden pray for the Jews and the heathen instead ; and perhaps it was better to let the prayer grow with her growth, for when she was older and became interested in them, of her own accord she prayed for both Jews and Gentiles ; and if she had been told that it was not proper to pray about such little things as kittens, she might next have doubted whether it was right for little things to pray.

Let the children's home be bright and beautiful and very gladsome. It was brightly that the existence of the race began ; and with all that you can do to embellish and enliven the nursery, it will not be so charming as the first place which our Heavenly Father prepared for His children : it will not come up to the garden God planted on the banks of Hiddekel. But when bleak days arrive, it is good to have sweet and sunny memories; for fancy gives them wings and sends them on before, and in the guise of hope they invite us into the future. What we call idealism is really Edenism : it is partly the reminiscence of one paradise, partly the effort after another. And in that home the very brightest, gladdest, holiest thing, let it be the name of Jesus, the presence of God. In psalms and hymns sweetly sung, in the going up to the house of God, in Sabbaths crowned with special joys, in Bible stories and good books, let there be not only the didactic but the endearing; and even if some loveless nature should be the sad exception, and pass through it all as sullen as that elder brother, it may well be hoped that few will ever wander; and if there should be some hapless prodigal, —carrying such recollections with him, who can doubt that in the far country they will at last awaken an irresistible longing, and end in exclaiming, "I will arise and go to my Father ?"

Be this your aim. Father, mother, brothers, sisters, as the years advance, join your efforts to upbuild and beautify the home. Let it be the abode of peace, and love, and mutual helpfulness, and let those nights be the happiest when no one needs to leave it.

" How calm, how blest this tranquil hour
    Of household evening joy !
The world shut out, with all its power
    To trouble or annoy.

" The world shut out, and love shut in,
    With youth and gentle mirth,
Which ever make their pleasant din
    Best by the household hearth.

" The duties of the day are done,
    Its toil and burden o'er,
To claim, until the rising sun,
    Our anxious hearts no more.

" Then let us rest amid the gifts
    God's tenderness hath given,
And bless each blessing as it lifts
    Our grateful hearts to heaven." *

A scene like that, a shadow of still better things, to the heart which has ever known it will be a charm for ever :—a magnet, the force of which will be felt across the hemisphere—a saving memory which in the darkest hour will sustain the wanderer's faith in goodness and in God.

                * Monsell.

A RIGHTEOUS FATHER.

N

"Therefore came his father out, and entreated him. And he answering said to his father, Lo, these many years do I serve thee, neither transgressed I at any time thy commandment; and yet thou never gavest me a kid, that I might make merry with my friends: but as soon as this thy son was come, which hath devoured thy living with harlots, thou hast killed for him the fatted calf. And he said unto him, Son, thou art ever with me, and all that I have is thine. It was meet that we should make merry and be glad: for this thy brother was dead, and is alive again; and was lost, and is found."—LUKE xv. 28-32.

HE WAS ANGRY, AND WOULD NOT GO IN; THEREFORE CAME HIS
FATHER OUT, AND ENTREATED HIM

A RIGHTEOUS FATHER.

Sketched by the hand of a Divine Artist, we have here a picture of fatherhood inimitable and unapproachable, and which inevitably sends up our thoughts to the Divine Original from which it is outlined. Fain would we dwell on it; but before passing away we merely notice

1. *The father's love.*—Of a kindred love the apostle declares that its breadth, and length, and depth, and height pass knowledge; and a great deep must have been that affection which the sharp wind of ingratitude failed to freeze, which a long course of waywardness could not exhaust, and of which, on the prodigal's return, the fountains broke up, and, overflowing in a grand final burst of compassion, covered mountains of provocation, leaving all things new at their reflux in the mind of the pardoned penitent.

2. *His wisdom.*—Our fondness sometimes grows foolish, and in concessions and refusals alike our weakness is shown. When the younger son demanded his portion of goods, though deeply wounded the father did not withstand. His home should not be a prison, and

where the highest considerations and holiest influences had lost their power, he would not resort to coercion. He foresaw the result, but as this was a folly which experience alone could cure, he allowed the truant to depart and find out for himself how hard is the way of transgressors. Nor did he shorten the trial. If, as is not unlikely, he knew of the famine in the far country, he took no steps to interpose betwixt the misguided youth and a severe but salutary discipline; till, thoroughly filled with the fruits of his own devices, he felt and owned the bitter evil of his sin.

3. *His dignity.*—In all the father's sayings, as well as in his silence, come out the tokens of a lofty mind. When the younger son demands his portion, the deed which wisdom dictates is performed with regal grandeur; no remonstrance, no unavailing entreaties, no attempt at compromise, nothing kept back in the way of deduction; and when he returns, a ragged and penniless outcast, there is no recalling of the past, no stipulation as to the future, but a forgiveness frank and free, a kingly munificence dissolving in fatherly tenderness, and from an ingenuous spirit the surest to draw back filial devotion. With like elevation he meets a rude remonstrance. In the coarseness of rage the elder son did not even address him as " father," and only spoke of his brother as " this thy son ;" but with high-born grace and the kindly tact of a goodness safe in its own supremacy, the father vindicates himself, and puts to shame the angry railer.

" Son "—for it is thus he retorts the insult which would not call him " father "—" Son, thou art ever with me, and all that I have is thine. It was meet that *we* [you and I and all of us] should make merry and be glad ; [and if any should be merrier than another it is thou] for this *thy brother* was dead, and is alive again ; and he was lost, and is found."

4. *His large-heartedness.*—Not only was he a generous householder, where the hired servants had bread enough and to spare ; but he could not be happy himself without giving others a share. " To the servants he had never told his grief ; but now the prodigal is come back, and his heart is bursting with joy, he tells them of it. He cannot conceal it, he does not seek to conceal it. He says, Let us eat and be merry—I am so happy myself, I wish all others to be happy. Banish all care ; drop your toils ; let the shepherd come from the hill, the ploughman from the furrow, the herd from the pastures, the meanest servant come ; and all wearing smiles, and joining in the song, hold holiday with my heart."*

5. *His equity.*—His elder son thought him unfair. " Here have I been toiling on these weary years, improving the estate and never causing thee a moment's anxiety : yet thou hast never given me so much as a kid with which to entertain my friends : but as soon as this thy son was come, who hath devoured thy living with harlots, thou hast killed for him the fatted calf." Angry and out-

* Dr. Guthrie.

spoken, this splenetic effusion betrayed a wretched spirit. Passing for a son, he had all along been actuated by feelings which many a hireling would blush to avow; and, "never receiving wages, he had certainly never yet enjoyed the only true reward in his heart."[*] After a speech so petulant and saucy, the father might have turned away in displeasure and left him to his wrathful musings; but in order to bring him to his right mind, in the tone most fitted to conquer and conciliate, he sets before the murmurer considerations which had escaped his evil eye. The question of work and wages was settled by that one word "Son," and is disposed of more completely still in the noble utterance, "All that I have is thine." Betwixt a father and a son there can be no separate interests. If desirous to entertain thy friends, there was not on all the estate kid or fatted calf which thou couldst not any day command. But there are higher equities than work and wages. Even as a labourer thou hast received thine hire; but when all accounts are settled we still owe love to one another: our debt to the highest charities it needs a lifetime to discharge. It is "meet" that we should forgive faults and injuries. It is meet that we should compassionate the wretched and receive the penitent. It is meet that we should fulfil the claims of affection, be it parental or fraternal; and when our hearts are filled with gladness it is meet that we should express our joy, and let our friends and neighbours share

* Van Oosterzee *On Luke,* vol. ii. p. 68.

it. It is meet that you and I should on a day like this make merry.

Let us hope that the entreaty was not in vain, and that, bringing to his right mind the elder son, this happy night closed over a completed family. For, as it now turns out, both sons had been lost. The one had run away, but the other was a truant in spirit though he tarried at home. And to give heart and soul to a loveless nature —to give loyalty and devotion to the calculating mercenary—to create the filial spirit where there was nothing but the name before, needs grace as mighty as that which heals backslidings and recals the wanderer, and sets among the princes the once abject and degraded prodigal.

A piece of gold may be melted, and it may be moulded into almost any shape. It may be rolled out in bars, drawn into wire, minted into money. It may be twisted into the finest filigree, or beaten into leaflets, compared with which the flimsiest fabric of the loom or paper-frame seems coarse. But if you are so fortunate as to find a goodly pearl, you will not apply pincers or hammer, nor will you put it in the crucible. You will do wisely to preserve its original form unaltered, its native lustre unimpaired.

Some texts are golden. In the arguments of the Epistles and in the devotional outpourings of the Psalms, as well as in the historical incidents of either Testament,

those who search the Scriptures will find great truths
imbedded; and, sectile, ductile, malleable, we feel that it
is no misuse if they are projected into propositions,
divided into heads and particulars, drawn out into mani-
fold applications, or even attenuated into such thin foil
as is used in the manufacture of modern theological
essays. A good deal may be done with a few grains of
gold; and in this field, faithful and persevering search is
sure to be rewarded with hoards or solid ingots.

There are other passages, however, which we dare
not thus handle. We may repeat them, and revolve
them, and, like gems, may hold them up in different
lights, or try them in various settings; but such a saying
as "God is love," and such an incident as our Lord's
lamentation over Jerusalem, we feel as if no scholastic tool
should ever touch them. What better can the preacher
do than exhibit them in their divine and unapproachable
glory to the reverential contemplation of his hearers, per-
adventure trying a few of those expedients which are open
to us in the way of foil and cross-light and contrast?

Such a feeling has kept us hovering timidly over this
"pearl of parables."* Unable to pass away from it, we

---

* An expression of Stier, quoted by Van Oosterzee, Alford, and
nearly all subsequent annotators. "For the beautiful, the pathetic, the
instructive," says Dr. Adam Clarke, "the history of Joseph in the Old
Testament, and the parable of the prodigal son in the New, have no
parallels either in sacred or profane history." Even the cold rational-
istic temperament of Grotius is thawed into a fervid admiration. "Inter
omnes Christi parabolas hæc sane eximia, plena affectuum, et pul-

have failed to expound it. We have thrown out a few
thoughts which its contemplation suggested, and noted a
few analogous incidents gleaned from the records of a
kindred experience. But the fair flower in your garden
you do not cut down and dissect; you rather return and
dwell on its loveliness day after day. And when people
speak of throwing light on such a passage, it almost seems
a preposterous inversion. Itself a light in a dark place,
as there it stands and from the lattice of the Father's house
shines toward our far country, its friendly radiance has
cheered and guided to the threshold many a benighted
wanderer. It needs no exposition. It only needs the
softened heart, the wistful gaze, the single eye. These
may He graciously bestow who is the Spirit of Truth and
Tenderness!

No doubt, from time to time as we proceeded, parallel
instances have recurred to the mind of many a reader.
Besides names already quoted, some would think of John
Newton and General Burn. To memories familiar with
early Christian records would recur the story of the youth
become a renegade and robber, so remarkably reclaimed

cherrimis picta coloribus." As has been well said by a living compatriot
of the great Hollander, "Nowhere is that divine compassion which an-
ticipates and outruns the sinner set forth in a way more tender and
human—I might say, in a way more sincere and affectionate—than in
this beautiful parable, which gives us deep insight into both the loving
heart of the Divine Father and the sinful heart of man (Gods liefderijk
vaderhart en het zondaarshart van den mensch)." Cohen-Stuart: *De
Verloren Zoon*, Utrecht, p. 7.

by the apostle John; and what are Augustine's Confessions but a long and yet intense expansion of the Prodigal's prayer? In the Pitcairn Islanders we have the departure and return of a prodigal ship's company; and the annals of reformations and religious revivals remind us of the Father's house forsaken and sought again by prodigal nations. A few individual examples may form an appropriate conclusion. They may comfort those who are mourning over a prodigal not yet returned. They illustrate the providence of God and the way of His Spirit. They are an encouragement to prayer, and on the side of parents and others they should be an incentive to personal exemplariness as long as the family circle continues unbroken.

During the late American war, at one of the Saturday evening meetings in Camp Distribution said a soldier to his comrades, " My friends, I left home an infidel, but I left a praying wife. A week ago I received a letter from her, in which she expressed anxiety for the welfare of my soul, and desired to know if I still held to my old views. I wrote an answer to the letter, and in bitter words defended my old position. As I was about to seal the letter, it seemed to me I could not send it. I wrote another, softened down considerably from the first, but when that was done I could not send it. I commenced another, but such was the power of the Spirit upon my heart, that I fell upon my knees and begged for forgiveness before God. I could not finish the letter until I could say to my dear wife that Christ had forgiven my sins. I have been permitted to write to her that I am to-night rejoicing in her Saviour. I feel that I am now prepared for the battle-field, and if ever I am permitted to return home, I trust I shall go back prepared for that, a better man than when I came into the army."* We hope the praying wife and the converted husband were soon allowed to meet; but sometimes these prayers are not answered till the supplicant has reached the land of praise. When Hedley Vicars was in Canada there was a young man in his Bible-class who sometimes felt a good deal touched by the earnest words of that fine Christian hero; but although almost persuaded, like most of his comrades he continued frolicsome, light-hearted, and god-less. They were ordered to the Crimea, and one dark night in the trenches the Russians made a sortie, and in repelling it Vicars fell with a rifle-ball through his heart. A bullet pierced through the heart of the captain, and at the same instant a sword went through the soul of the young soldier. The captain, he felt, has gone to heaven; but where shall I go if there be a like messenger for me? The words which his fallen chief had spoken whilst yet with them were now called to remembrance, and ended in the entire revolution of his feelings and character.—It was from the lips of the Crimean soldier himself that we heard the tale, and he had then become a diligent and faithful Christian minister.

* *Fourth Annual Report of the United States Christian Commission*, p. 77.

The far country is wide, and to those who try to follow the prodigal its recesses are intricate, its fastnesses very inaccessible. But although the remonstrances of a father, the tears of a sister, the silent beseechings of a broken-hearted wife, may never overtake the wanderer; although, shut up in the iron fortress of his own passion or self-pleasing, he may defy them all, and throw them off as the adamant sheds the hail-shower, there is One who compasses the path of the prodigal, and from whose presence it is idle to flee. We told how a prodigal's progress was arrested in the case of George Cowie of Huntly. On the authority of his biographer, we venture to relate an incident still more striking in the career of the illustrious American missionary, Adoniram Judson. He was a minister's son, and, very able and very ambitious, he was early sent to college. In the class above was a young man of the name of E——, brilliant, witty, and popular, but a determined deist. Between him and the minister's son there sprang up a close intimacy, which ended in the latter gradually renouncing all his early beliefs, and becoming as great a sceptic as his friend. He was only twenty years of age, and you may be sure it was a terrible distress and consternation which filled the home circle, when, during the recess, he announced that he was no longer a believer in Christianity. More than a match for his father's arguments, he steeled himself against all softer influences, and with his mind made up to enjoy life and see the world, he first joined a company of players at

New York, and then set out on a solitary tour. One night he stopped at a country inn. Lighting him to his room, the landlord mentioned that he had been obliged to place him next door to a young man who was exceedingly ill, in all probability dying, but he hoped that it would occasion him no uneasiness. Judson assured him that, beyond pity for the poor sick man, he should have no feeling whatever. Still the night proved a restless one. Sounds came from the sick chamber—sometimes the movements of the watchers, sometimes the groans of the sufferer—and the young traveller could not sleep. So close at hand, with but a thin partition between us, he thought, there is an immortal spirit about to pass into eternity, and is he prepared? And then he thought, "For shame of my shallow philosophy! What would E——, so intellectual and clear-headed, think of this boyish weakness?" And then he tried to sleep, but still the picture of the dying man rose up to his imagination. He was a "young man," and the young student felt compelled to place himself on his neighbour's dying bed, and he could not help fancying what, in such circumstances, would be his thoughts. But the morning dawned, and in the welcome daylight his "superstitious illusions" fled away. When he came down stairs he inquired of the landlord how his fellow-lodger had passed the night. "He is dead," was the answer. "Dead!" "Yes; he is gone, poor fellow! The doctor said he would probably not survive the night." "Do you know who he was?"

"Oh, yes; it was a young man from Providence College —a very fine fellow; his name was E——." Judson was completely stunned. Hours passed before he could quit the house; but when he did resume his journey, the words "Dead! lost! lost!" were continually ringing in his ears. There was no need for argument. God had spoken, and from the presence of the living God the chimeras of unbelief and the pleasures of sin alike fled away. The religion of the Bible he knew to be true; and turning his horse's head towards Plymouth, he rode slowly homewards, his plans of enjoyment all shattered, and ready to commence that rough and uninviting path which, through the death-prison at Ava and its rehearsal of martyrdom, conducted to the grave at Maulmain.[*]

Our last example we take from the proceedings of a Society which has rescued many a wandering youth, and prevented many more from becoming prodigals. The class which the young foreigner attended was conducted by a dear friend of our own, and it was thus that at a meeting of the Young Men's Christian Association the circumstances were not long ago narrated :—"Nine years ago a young Frenchman presented himself for relief, requesting medicine and assistance. He was wretchedly poor, without food, almost without clothes, a deserter from the French army, and in consequence unable to revisit his native country; and even here, he went in terror that by some means he might be arrested, and made to suffer

[*] See Wayland's *Life of Judson*, vol. i. p. 12.

for his fault. The medicine for which he asked the chemist gave him, and for relief he was directed to the Young Men's Christian Association. He came on Easter Sunday 1855, and found here the welcome with which you are always ready to greet a stranger who comes to throw himself upon your sympathy. He was placed under the care of a Christian gentleman, and under his guidance and teaching he learned the great truths of Christianity, and resolved to devote himself to the service of God. He continued for some time to attend your meetings, which were the source of much benefit to him; but in his altered state of mind he considered it was his first duty to make what reparation he could for the fault of which he had been guilty in deserting his regiment. He returned to France, presented himself to the proper officers, and surrendered himself as a deserter. On his trial much surprise was expressed at his voluntary surrender of himself, and the president specially interrogated him on this point. He replied: 'When I ran away from France I was in the darkness of nature, and under the power of sin; now I have learned the gospel of the Lord Jesus Christ, and am His servant. It is by the teaching of His Word that I come back to my duty, and submit myself to you for the punishment I have deserved.' Kind friends took an interest in his welfare, and tried to procure a mitigation of his punishment. They were successful. Twelve years' punishment was the ordinary penalty for his offence; this was reduced to four, and the severity of the imprisonment greatly mitigated. After undergoing it for a year and nine months, he was allowed to return to duty in the army. Here he was employed as a sort of regimental clerk for about two years, and then finally granted a discharge. Released from all obligation, he went to Geneva to study for the ministry. When his studies were completed, he laboured for some time in the south of France as an evangelist, and then was appointed to the charge of the French Independent Church at Guernsey. He now stands before you to acknowledge that this happy change of position, and far happier change of mind, he owes to the kindly influence of the Young Men's Christian Association. The starving French deserter who sang in the streets of London for a morsel of bread, is the Pastor M——, who now speaks to you."

INDEX.

ACTIVITY essential to enduring enjoyment, 159
Addison, 148
Advocate, story of an Edinburgh, 109
Affliction, sobering uses of, 102
Alexander's " Thoughts," 77
Alfieri, anecdote of, 137
Alford, 149
Alison's " French Revolution," 13
Apologues : Abdallah and the expanding imp, 28 ; the Happy Isle, 141
Aratus, 5
Arnold's, Dr., sister, 96
Arnot on the Parables, 150
Augustine's experience, 139
" Aurora Leigh," 133
Aytoun's " Bothwell," 61

BARNES on Isaiah, 10
Basilisk, the, 101
Beattie's Life of Campbell, 27
Bible expositors, 147
Blake, Wm., and the angels, 173
Bradford's farewell letter, 22
" Brand plucked from the burning," 104

Brother, an angry, 161 ; who is he ? 164
Brown's " Home Life," 172
Brummell, George, 89
Bunyan, 71
Burns, 54
Byron, 76

CALVIN, 147
Candlish's " Fatherhood," 119
Charles of Bala, 151
Chatterton, 71
Childhood : its advantages in a Christian home, 136 ; how to make it beautiful and happy, 174
Children of Christian parents turn out well, 9 ; training of, 12 ; lost in Australian wilderness, 120 ; educators of parents, 132 ; have no turn for abstraction, 132 ; acute observers, 133 ; rich in imagination, 173
Christ, love to, 94 ; mediation of, 115 ; the manifestation of God, 116
Clarke, Dr. A., quoted, 184
Cleopatra's pearl, 55
Cohen-Stuart quoted, 185
Colton, career of Caleb, 91

Commentators, early, 147
Companions, choice of, 24, 62
Conversion of Vanderkemp, 105 ; of W. Howard, 139 ; of an American soldier, 186 ; of Judson, 188 ; of a French deserter, 190
Cords of love, 4
Country, the far, 33
Cowie of Huntly, 19
Cowper, 156
Crewdson, Mrs., quoted, 166

DANTE, 83
Dobell's " Balder," 6
Dwight's " Sermons," 123

EGYPT, 38
Erasmus, 147
Evans's " Frauds," etc., 58
Exile's home-longing, 4

FABER, F. W., 135
Famine, a mighty, 65
Father, a righteous, 177
Fatherhood of God, 118, 125 ; as portrayed by Jesus Christ, 179
Fatherland, the, 1
Feeding swine, 81
" Felix Holt," 101
Festival, the, 145
Flowers, children who had never seen, 172
" Friends in Council," 169

GAMBLING, 43
Gifts, diversity of, 156
God (see Fatherhood), His disposi-
tion towards the repenting sinner, 122 ; His mercy not hindered by His holiness, 123
Goethe's mother, 14
Gospels, great and small, 77
Greswell, 149
Grimshaw, 51
Grotius, 147
Gustavus Adolphus, 158
Guthrie, Dr., 181

HABITS, bad, 27
Hamilton, Lady, 92
Happiness of Christians, 141
Harris's " Patriarchy," 8
Henry's Exposition, 148
Herodotus, 87
Home, the true, of humanity, God, 6 ; image of the church, 8 ; leaving, 17 ; the first made by God, 172
Hooper, 60
Howard's, William, conversion, 139
Husks, 88

IDEALISM ; its uses, 26
Impracticable people, 169
Income, keep within the, 62
Intemperance, 55
Isle, the Happy, 141

JAMES, J. A. : the Bible in his pocket, 21 ; dying testimony, 152
Jay's happiness in life, 95
Judson, 188

KIRBY, the entomologist, 14
Kirke White, 21
Krummacher, Daniel, anecdote of, 165

LADIES, work of Christian, 158

Laffitte ; how he made his fortune, 68

Lawrence, Amos, on starting "just right," 30

Livingstone, Dr. D., quoted, 173 ; John, 135

Lorelei, the, 44

Lost, joy in finding the, 119

Love, identity of all true, 170

Loveless natures, 168

Lytton, Lord, quoted, 21 .

MACDONALD, Dr., 157

Maclaren's "Sermons," 117

Manhood, true, 51

Masson's "Essays," 73

Meeting, a happy, 113

Melancthon's early piety, 134

Milner, Joseph, 130

Milton, 51

Monsell, 176

Montgomery, 55

Moore's Life of Byron, 78

Murray, Dr. N., and the old man, 158

NAPOLEON and the English sailor, 13 ; his mother, 14 ;

Nisbet, Mr., anecdote of, 45

OLSHAUSEN quoted, 149

Oosterzee, Van, 182, 184

PEACE with God—how obtained, 144

Porson, 63

Pringle, T., 25

Prodigal, the ; his original abode, 35 ; leaves it, 37 ; new scenes and sensations, 41 : squanders his fortune, 48 ; in want, 86 ; feeding swine, 87 ; comes to himself, 100; comes home, 128

Profusion, 84

QUAKER, the ; how he made his money, 68

RAIKES, R., 156

Resolution, a wise, 97

Riotous living, 49

Robe, the best, 129 ; its significance, 149, *note*

Rogers, the martyr's, descendants, 10

SANDEMAN, D., 93

Savage, Richard, 92

Shakspere, 88

Sheridan, 54

Sin, struggle with, 138 ; distinction between sins brute-like and fiend-like, 74

Spendthrifts, 83

Stier quoted, 166, 184

Stork, the, 4

Swindler's, the, progress, 57 ; another 58

Swine in Egypt, 87

TAYLOR, JEREMY, 156

Temptation, 138

Thiersch and his mother, 15

Traveller's, the, dangers and duties 39, 43

Trench quoted, 149

UNCLEAN spirit wandering through dry places, 73

Usefulness, various ways of, 154

VANCOUVER Indian and Sturgeon, 55

Vanderkemp, 105

Variety in God's kingdom, 155 ; in the minds of men, 156 ; in gifts and ministrations, 157

WHITFIELD, 157

Wife, a, 15

Wilkinson's "Ancient Egypt," 87

Wordsworth, 6

THE END.

www.ingramcontent.com/pod-product-compliance
Lightning Source LLC
Chambersburg PA
CBHW030117030726
47498CB00007B/2425